BACKSTAGE AT THE METS

BACKSTAGE AT THE METS

by LINDSEY NELSON

with AL HIRSHBERG

The Viking Press

New York

First published in 1966 by The Viking Press, Inc.
625 Madison Avenue, New York, N.Y. 10022

Published simultaneously in Canada by
The Macmillan Company of Canada Limited

Library of Congress catalog card number: 66–15881
Printed in U.S.A. by The Colonial Press

To—   .   .
Edna and Casey

CONTENTS

BACKSTAGE AT THE METS

"We'll Knock 'Em Dead in New York"

AND there I was, swinging back and forth like a monkey in a cage, under the roof of the Astrodome in Houston. Second base was 208 feet below me. The ballplayers, only the tops of their heads visible, looked like animated pushbuttons. From where I sat with our executive producer, Joel Nixon, they might have been playing marbles. At the moment I didn't have the foggiest notion what they were doing, where they were going, or why.

It was a perfect spot for a New York Mets announcer.

I suppose this was, in a way, my comeuppance for a fresh bit of doggerel verse I had produced at the 1965 baseball dinner given by the governor of Florida in Tampa less than a month before. As master of ceremonies, I had spoofed a number of things, including Judge Roy Hofheinz, the verbose president of the Houston ball club, who had dreamed up the Astrodome.

The Hofheinz canto of Nelson's Elegy in a Tampa Banquet Hall ran:

> And in Houston now a dome
> That the Astros call their home,
> Air-conditioned, simply lovely, it's a peach.
> And if the air should chill,
> There is heat, without a bill,
> Simply introduce Judge Hofheinz for a speech.

If Judge Hofheinz now chortled, it was only his right. And, as he leaned back in the plush comfort of his solid gold box while I hung on for dear life in a mesh gondola high above his head, he must have been chortling. What a way to get even!

Of course the judge had nothing to do with my unhappy perch. I had nobody but myself to blame—or practically nobody. The whole thing was the brainchild of our producer, Joe Gallagher. I had the dim wit to go along with him. Let's face it, I broke a cardinal rule that four years in the Army in World War II had failed to get through to me. I volunteered.

We arrived in Houston from San Francisco, where the Mets had stunned us all by taking three out of four games from the Giants. As we walked through the Houston airport somebody approached Manager Casey Stengel (somebody was always approaching Casey Stengel) and said, "Pardon me, Casey. You don't know me. I'm just a fan, but I've followed you and the Mets, and I wonder how you feel about playing in the Astrodome."

"The Astrodome," Casey said. "The Astrodome. Why, Soboda'll knock the top off that thing!"

We couldn't wait for our first look at the place. Neither could Jim Murray, the Los Angeles *Times* columnist. He was so anxious to see it he headed home from New York via Houston. He phoned us at the Shamrock-Hilton right after we checked in. I told him to come on over.

Jim is an old friend of mine. I think one of his finest hours must have come on an icy night in St. Paul, Minnesota, in about 1956. With an evening to kill before a football game, he and I went to a movie together. As, surrounded by women in mink coats and men in Brooks Brothers creations, we shivered in the lobby of the theater, he shook his head and whispered, "These poor, poor people!"

"What's poor about them?" I asked.

"Tomorrow you'll be back in New York and I'll be back in Los Angeles, but they'll still be in Saint Paul," he said.

My Met broadcasting partners, Ralph Kiner and Bob Murphy, were with me in the lobby of the Shamrock when Murray arrived. In the cab somebody told the driver to take us to "the Hofheinz palace." The driver knew what we meant. In Houston, whenever you say "Hofheinz" you mean "Astrodome." Its real title is the Harris County Domed Stadium, but, except for the local newspapers, nobody calls it that.

We spent the afternoon looking over this fantastic structure, which attracted seven thousand sightseers a day at a dollar a head, just to tour the place. The team hadn't drawn that many people for ball games before the Astrodome was built.

Instead of going around with Kiner, Murphy, and Murray, I would have been smarter to keep my eye on Joe Gallagher. A former statistician for the New York Yankees, before graduating to the Columbia Broadcasting System as a producer en route to his job with the Mets, he was always looking for something new and different. His eyes must have gleamed when he discovered the gondola nestled beneath the roof of the Astrodome.

I heard later what happened.

"Does that thing move?" Joe asked.

"Sure," an Astrodome official replied. "You can lower it right to the ground. We figured photographers and newsreel men might like to use it for certain events. It would be especially good for fights."

"Has it ever been used for a ball game?"

"I don't know how it could be," the official said. "It would get in the way of the game."

"Not if it stayed where it is," Joe said. "Any way of getting up to it?"

"There's a catwalk. Or the gondola could be lowered to pick somebody up, and then raised up to the top again."

"Um," Joe ummed. I can hear him now.

During the ball game that night he kept looking up at the top of the dome. Once I heard him say, "You know, it would be a hell of a thing to do a broadcast from up there."

This went in one ear and out the other. I was all wrapped up in the ball game. The Mets had a one-run lead, with the Astros up in the last of the ninth. Houston got two men on base, with two out and Eddie Kasko up. Dennis Ribant, a young right-hander with a lot of nervous energy, was pitching in relief for the Mets. I hoped Ribant could save the game for Jack Fisher, who had done a fine job until he tired in the ninth. Besides, if the Mets could win this one after their big series in San Francisco, they might gather momentum and go on and on and on . . .

Ah me, the dreams you dream when you have followed the Mets as long and as closely as I have!

Ribant got two strikes on Kasko, putting himself just one strike away from glorious victory. Out there on the mound, he was all business. So was I.

"Ribant steps off the rubber," I said into the mike. "He kicks at the dirt, tugs at his sleeve, rubs up the ball. He looks around the outfield, glances at the men on base, then turns in

towards the plate. He mops his brow, pulls at the bill of his
cap, toes the rubber, looks in for the sign, nods his head . . . he's
up and set . . . off the stretch . . . takes a last look at the runner
on third and—here's the pitch. . . . Kasko swings. . . . It's a
fly ball deep to left. Joe Christopher is coming over . . . full
speed . . . he's reaching, he's reaching . . ." I saw he wasn't
going to make it, but I tried to keep my voice up.

"He can't get it," I said. "The ball lands on the warning track
and takes one hop to the wall. Both runners score, and the
game is over. Houston wins."

It was a nice try, a stunning loss for the Mets. The season
was new, they had just wrecked the Giants, and they hoped
that those days of losing in the late innings were behind them,
that those weird endings were a thing of the past. Dreams, all
dreams.

The next afternoon I went over to station KPRC to cut some
tapes, then returned to the hotel. The whole Met broadcasting
crew—Nixon, Gallagher, Kiner, Murphy, and I—had a luxurious
five-room suite, complete with master bedroom, kitchen, serving
pantry, living room, and attendant bedrooms. These were not,
I might add, our usual accommodations. However, there was a
big convention in town, and the manager didn't have anywhere
else to put us. He apologized for "crowding" us all together. I'll
settle for that kind of crowding any time.

The only one in when I arrived from the broadcasting station
was Gallagher, draped around a telephone as usual. He was
talking to somebody about that gondola. When I heard him
ask about lowering it to second base, I should have walked out.
Instead, I was reminded of Frank Slocum's classic remark
during the winter baseball meetings in Houston.

When Slocum, one of Commissioner Ford Frick's assistants,
was taken on the tour of the Astrodome, his guide dutifully
reported, "The Astrodome is eighteen stories high. The
Shamrock-Hilton could be set inside the dome at second base

and not touch the top."

Whereupon Frank commented, "Yes, but how would they make the double play?"

Gallagher finished talking on the phone and turned to me. "That was the Astrodome," he said. "They're going to call me back."

He walked over to a plush divan and stretched out on it, his hands clasped behind his head. "I got everything fixed with the telephone company," he said. "They'll put a line into the gondola, although that took a little doing. They were afraid when it gets lowered it might pull the line out, but there's really no problem. All they have to do is terminate the line in the stationary part of the structure up by the roof, and we can connect it up after the gondola gets back up there. The microphone could be plugged in, and we'd be all set."

"For what?" I asked in tones much like those I used announcing Kasko's hit the night before.

"We're going to broadcast from there tonight."

"Are we?"

"Yeah, if we get permission. That's what I'm waiting for now."

He peered so hard at me that I looked the other way. I wished either Kiner or Murphy, or both, were around. It seemed to me this was a situation that could stand a little talking over.

"Y'know, Lindsey," Joe said, "it's going to be real embarrassing if, after all the arguing and arranging I've done, I get that permission, and the gondola is lowered in front of all those people, and I suddenly discover that we don't have anybody to go up in it."

"I guess it will," I said.

"If they call back and say we can do it, I've got to tell them right now who we're sending up."

I went to the window—as far away from Gallagher as I could get. We faced the Texas Medical Center, a huge complex of hospitals a few blocks from the hotel. I looked out, vaguely wondering which building they'd take me to if I fell out of a gondola.

Joe, still staring hypnotically at me, hadn't stopped talking. ". . . and I did raise a terrible stink. I told them of course we wanted to do a game from up there, and what was wrong with that? I met every objection with a sound answer. They didn't think a broadcast was possible, and they probably still don't."

He paused. Then he said, "Of course, we won't be able to do one without an announcer. They'll be calling any minute, and I have to tell them somebody."

I finally turned, met his gaze, and shrugged. "Tell you, Joe," I said. "At my time of life I'm not exactly crazy about trying out new forms of transportation. But if you *do* get the gondola down, and if you *are* stuck for somebody to go up and broadcast from it, I suppose I *would* go."

If Joe had even a token protest on the tip of his tongue, he never had time to express it, for at that very moment the phone rang. He answered it, listened a minute, and grinned.

"Fine, that's fine," he said. "Bring it down at seven o'clock, and Lindsey Nelson will go up and do the broadcast. Joel Nixon will go with him. You'll get plenty of publicity. The New York press is here with our ball club, and we'll be broadcasting back to New York on the Met network."

After Joe hung up I said, "Have you asked Joel to go up?"

"Well—no," Gallagher said. "But maybe he won't object. Now Lindsey," he went on, "you guys will have to stay up there for the whole game. It takes about six minutes to bring the gondola down and six more to get it up again. I can't think of any time during the game we'd have twelve minutes to make the round trip."

"Unless it rains," I remarked.

"In the Astrodome? Be careful what you eat and drink, by the way. There's no men's room up there."

"Yeah," I said.

"Of course there's that catwalk. It clings to a girder and leads over to the side of the building, where you could make an exit in an emergency. Only it's pretty hazardous."

"Yeah."

"Lindsey, it will be a great experience, something you can tell your grandchildren about. And we'll knock 'em dead in New York."

"Yeah."

Joe slapped me on the back, and I smiled a sick smile.

At the Astrodome, the managers of the two ball clubs agreed to move up the schedule of batting and fielding practice enough to allow time for us to get up in the gondola. It began its descent a few minutes after seven. As it came down a sign was flashed on the electric message board in center field, reading: "The gondola is being lowered to pick up Lindsey Nelson, who will broadcast part of the game back to New York from the top of the dome."

Yogi Berra read the sign and came over to me in front of the Mets dugout. "You gonna go up in that thing?" he demanded.

"Yes."

He stared at me, as if trying to look through me to find out what made me tick. Then he shook his head and said, "I think you're crazy." As I watched the gondola slowly come to a swaying stop about twelve feet above second base, I was inclined to agree.

Joel Nixon and I walked toward it. He was carrying a couple of walkie-talkies and a microphone, and he didn't look too happy.

"Joe asked if I wanted to be floor manager for the broadcast," he said, "and, like a dope, I said I would."

There were several men standing under the gondola when we got there. A couple were setting up a stepladder. Another said, "Don't worry about a thing. That gondola is held up by five cables. If any two should break, the other three will hold."

"I hope you're right," I said. "Only it's been my experience that when those things break, they break in bunches."

Somebody helped Joel up the ladder, then sort of tumbled him into the gondola because the last step wasn't quite high enough for anyone to reach it. When it was my turn, I started up as though these were the thirteen steps to the gallows. I'm a guy who is sorry they ever took running boards off automobiles. I like the comfort of that extra step.

One of the men handed us a couple of locker stools to sit on, and I yelled out to him, "Have you ever been up there?"

"Up there?" he yelled back. "You think I'm nuts?"

The next thing I knew we were headed domeward, while off in the distance we could hear the cheers of about twenty-eight thousand fans. The roar became louder as we moved up, for sound and heat rise in the Astrodome.

We were still going up when we heard Joe Gallagher on the walkie-talkie. "Stand by," he said.

"What else can I do?" I said.

We reached the top, and Joel plugged in the telephone line.

"We're on the air," Ralph Kiner announced.

"I'm in it," I said.

"What's it like up there, Lindsey?"

"They all look like midgets."

As the gondola came to rest, the cables tensed, and we could hear a lot of popping and crackling. I wondered what would happen next. I was sitting on my stool, looking over the steel railing, which was about waist-high. The motors groaned and ground, and the popping and the crackling grew louder. I had visions of the whole works giving way, catapulting us both right back to second base, but the noise suddenly stopped and we were locked into place.

With one hand on the railing and the other on the microphone, I was hanging on for dear life. People were waving, and Joel suggested it might be a good idea for me to wave back, but I wasn't interested.

"I'm not letting go of anything," I said. "But I would like to stretch my legs a little."

I put one foot on the mesh flooring, then gave an exploratory lean. The mesh moved, and I quickly drew my foot back. I learned later that this was perfectly normal, for the flooring was built to give a little, but I wasn't about to find out how much. If I had an urge to exercise, this was one night I'd have to forget it.

Joel looked so still I was worried about him. "Are you all right?" I asked.

"I guess so," he said. "Only I have acrophobia."

"*Acrophobia?* Then what in heaven's name are you doing up here?"

"I thought this might cure it," he said.

"A Met," I muttered, "through and through."

I looked down on the field. The game was about to start, and there was a cluster around home plate—Casey Stengel, Manager Lum Harris of the Astros, and the umpires. Somebody was waving his arms around. It had to be Casey, of course.

Later, he told me what happened. The umpires hadn't seen the gondola go up. When they finished talking about the conventional ground rules, Casey said, "All right now, what about my man up there?"

"What man?" asked Tom Gorman, the chief umpire.

"My man, my man Lindsey up there."

"Up where?"

Casey pointed to the gondola and said, "Up there, in that cage under the roof."

Gorman scratched his head and said, "Any ball that hits the top of the dome is in play, so I suppose any ball that hits Lindsey is in play."

"Well," Casey said, "my man is a ground rule. That's the first time my man was ever a ground rule."

He was quite right. I had never been a ground rule before. But I had never broadcast a game from fair territory before, either.

The game began, but at first I couldn't see anything except a lot of tiny figures. Everybody looked the same height, and everybody looked short. The first ball hit was a line drive, but I soon found out that anything hit into the air looked the same from up where we were. You couldn't tell a line drive from a pop fly or a long, towering belt.

Now Bob Murphy was at the other end of the walkie-talkie. We talked back and forth about what I could see from the gondola and what was going on in the ball game. I could see everything except what happened at a blind spot in the outfield, where the gondola got in the way. But I had to identify the players by positions, because it was impossible to make out their numbers.

I started to keep a scorecard, then realized that my pencil could be a dangerous missile if I dropped it, so I put it in my pocket. I would have to keep track of the game from the scoreboard.

Each team got a run in the first inning. The Mets knocked out Bob Bruce, the Astros' starting pitcher, when they collected three runs in the top of the second.

"Nice lead," Murphy said. "I hope they can . . . corner of Texas and Main . . ."

"What did you say, Murph?" I asked.

"I said I hope they can hold that three-run lead."

"I mean about Texas and Main."

"I didn't say anything about Texas and Main."

"I could have sworn—" I began.

Over the walkie-talkie a voice cut in with, ". . . four-two-two, the Sheraton-Lincoln . . ."

Then it dawned on me. We were on the same wavelength with a cab company.

Cab drivers, dispatchers, Murphy, Kiner, and ballplayers weren't the only competitors for my attention. The nuclear ship *Savannah* was in town and the off-duty crew, cheering madly for the Mets, was in the Astrodome. A banner, "*Savannah* Bets on the Mets," stretched across the front of the section where the sailors sat. A bugler—well, a guy who tooted on a bugle—gave raucous encouragement whenever the spirit moved him, which was most of the time. He was so bad that even the electric scoreboard got into the act. At one point, after he collapsed on two notes leading a "Charge!" the board flashed a sign reading: "The *Savannah* bugler is way off key, the way we hope the Mets will be."

The Mets needed that like a hole in the head. They could go off key under their own power. By the fourth inning, when the Astros knocked the Mets' starting pitcher, Frank Lary, out of the box, they had blown not one but two three-run leads, and by the fifth they were behind 6–5. But they rallied for four runs in the sixth, when Houston needed three pitchers to get them out, so when the Astros came to bat in the last of the sixth the Mets were ahead by three runs again. This time the score was 9–6.

In the meantime, while getting used to the gondola, I became aware of just about every sound in the ball park. The umpire's voice came booming up like a cannon shot as he called balls and strikes. So did the yelling of coaches and ballplayers, from the dugouts as well as the field. These sounds and the notes of the *Savannah*'s bugler pierced through the normal crowd noises except when something happened that brought everyone, yelling and whistling and clapping, to his feet at once. Then we were engulfed in sound waves which gathered momentum as they rose to the roof. If noise alone could have shaken the gondola loose, Joel and I would have reached second base before the ballplayers did.

The cab drivers and I continued to share the walkie-talkie with Kiner or Murphy, and both the latter continued to be mystified at my failure to understand them all the time. They could hear me down in the booth, but they couldn't hear the cabbies. Apparently I was the star performer of the night, because the drivers could also hear me. They kept asking the dispatcher to repeat his orders. When they accused him of operating from the ball park, he thought they were nuts, because *he* couldn't hear me.

The confusion that resulted from this and all the racket in the gondola would have given an ordinary man the screaming-meemies, but I'm not an ordinary man. I'm a Met fan, and with us Met fans confusion is a way of life. So is cacophony. I was getting that from all directions. Come listen with me:

"Lindsey, Cisco is in . . . strike one . . . charge! . . . no show at the Southland . . . where do you want me to go now? . . . Cisco, I said . . . can't you hear me? . . . the passenger's name is Johnson, not Cisco . . . ball two . . . come on, come on . . . I'm trying to find out who's in the bullpen . . . get this guy outta there . . . strike two . . . charge! . . . let's go, Mets . . . I don't see anybody at the Little Club . . . Lindsey, look at the scoreboard . . . it's two and two now . . . how can you work from the ball park? . . . charge!. . . . I told you there's nobody at the Southland . . . what the hell is going on anyhow? . . ."

Confusion in the air was matched by confusion on the field. The Mets couldn't stand prosperity. Galen Cisco, who started the sixth, couldn't get anybody out. When he filled the bases with a hit and two passes, Stengel yanked him for young Tug McGraw, who quickly walked two men home. Al Jackson finally came in and put the fire out, but not before the Astros had collected four runs to regain the lead, 10–9. It was the third time in six innings the Mets had blown a three-run lead.

Up to this point I had been on the air back to New York only to do color. This consisted of questions from the booth and answers from me. When the disastrous sixth inning ended, Gallagher asked me if I could see enough to do the play-by-play. I could see enough, but I was hearing too much. Still, by just plunging ahead, I managed to ignore the cab drivers, the bugler, the dispatcher, and everything else that had been pounding my eardrums all night. When the ball was hit into the air I had to refer to the booth because I couldn't tell its height or probable destination. Otherwise, I got along pretty well. I did two innings, the seventh and the eighth, but all I brought the Mets was more trouble. The Astros scored two more runs in the eighth for a 12–9 victory.

The game was over, but most people stayed in their seats because Bill Giles, the Astros' publicity director, had put a sign up on the message board reading: "Lindsey Nelson will make his re-entry in just a moment."

I learned later that Bob Hope, who had dropped in for his first look at the Astrodome, got a note just then from Judge Hofheinz, inviting him to inspect Hofheinz's apartment. Hope's reply was, "I'll go in just a minute, but first I want to see if Lindsey really does make his re-entry."

Joel disconnected the telephone plug, and then came the moaning and groaning of the mechanism releasing us from the roof. It made a frightening racket, but by hanging on tight we managed not to panic when the gondola started its swaying descent. As we passed Judge Hofheinz's box somebody yelled, "How was it up there, Lindsey?" After four hours under the rafters, I was all out of noise. I couldn't even wave.

I really shifted position for the first time all evening after the gondola stopped. As I climbed over the rail, I reached with my foot for the top of the stepladder. By then, people were cheering and waving, and I loved every minute of it.

I was met on the ground by a neatly dressed man who shook hands with me and asked, "How was the temperature up there? Much hotter than here?"

"Quite a bit," I said. "It got hotter as we went along."

"How did it feel coming down? Was it obviously getting cooler as you descended?"

"Oh, yes."

"The reason I'm asking," the man said, "is that our people installed the air-conditioning equipment, and I was just wondering about it."

"Why don't you go there and see for yourself?" I suggested.

He stared at me, then demanded, "Do you think I'm out of my mind?"

I was feeling pretty good as we headed for the booth to pick up my bag and head for the airport. Who else had gone up in that gondola? In the booth I met Sandy Alper, our engineer from the WHN staff in New York. He was packing up his gear.

"Sandy," I said, "that was a fine microphone installation up there. How did they fix it up so well?"

"I fixed it."

"*You* fixed it? How could you do that from down here?"

"I went up there this afternoon," Sandy said.

"In the gondola?"

"No. I crawled across the catwalk up under the roof."

"You mean you *walked*?"

"Well," he said, "there wasn't any other way of getting up there."

I was crushed. It was like landing on the moon in a space capsule only to discover that somebody else had shinned up on a pole the week before.

Chapter 2

Me
and
Ronald
Colman

YOU'LL find Met fans everywhere. With apologies to Winston Churchill, they are on the seas and on the oceans, in the air and on the beaches, on the landing grounds and in the fields, in the streets and in the hills. When President John F. Kennedy visited Berlin in 1963, he was greeted by huge crowds waving banners in English and German. Pictures of him in the midst of these crowds were circulated throughout the world, with many of the banners plainly visible. To the delight of our public-relations director, the late Tom Meany, one read, "Let's go, Mets."

My training for the Mets began at birth, when my parents named me Lindsey after a family friend. I'm the youngest of three children. My sister and brother both had middle names, but I got short-changed in that department. Going through life with a name like Lindsey Nelson can result in all sorts of complications.

I didn't know until I reached school age that Lindsey was such a common last name my teachers thought it was mine. All through grammar school they called me Nelson, thinking that was my first name. My college professors called me "Mr. Lindsey." When my brother Jim and I went places together we were often referred to as the "Lindsey boys." I didn't mind, but it irked him no end.

Because "Lindsey" is not the usual spelling of the name, I often get messages and letters addressed to "Lindsay" Nelson. I never knew the difference until a few years ago. When I was at a meeting of the President's Council for Youth Fitness at Annapolis, Maryland, the Commissioner of Education told me that "Lindsey" is of English derivation and "Lindsay" of Scottish.

One of the National Hockey League's brightest stars for years was Ted Lindsay of the Detroit Red Wings. When Red Grange and I were football-broadcasting partners, we checked into a motel at Ann Arbor the night before a Michigan game. Grange, of course, was one of football's all-time greats. When he was on television regularly his face was nearly as familiar to sports fans as his name.

But not at Ann Arbor. In the motel restaurant where we went for breakfast the next morning, the proprietor ignored Grange and devoted all his attention to me. He opened the door, gasped, spread out his arms, and cried, "Ted Lindsay! Come in, Ted. You and your friend sit anywhere you want."

He followed us to our table, called a waitress over, and told her, "Give Ted anything he wants, and make the service special." He practically bowed his way out, then came back a few minutes later with a ledger-type book. He opened it to an empty page and said, "Ted, would you mind signing my book?"

"Not at all," I said.

In large script I wrote: "Lindsey Nelson, NBC." He looked at it, smiled, closed the book, and said, "Gee, Ted, thanks a lot."

Right after Yogi Berra became a Met coach he attended a dinner staged by the Long Island Mets Boosters in Huntington. The master of ceremonies introduced me as the Met announcer and asked if I would interview Yogi—just a few questions. Berra began his answer to the first question with, "Well, Lindsey . . ." but on the next one he replied, "Well, Ted . . ." He called me Ted for the remainder of the interview, and he calls me Ted to this day. Yogi, like the Ann Arbor restaurant proprietor, is an ardent hockey fan.

After John V. Lindsay announced his candidacy for mayor of New York, a fan approached me in the Shea Stadium parking lot just before I got into my car one night. "Lindsey," he said, "I've been a Democrat all my life, but I'm going to vote for you."

"Thanks a lot," I said. It was much easier than trying to explain. It hasn't happened yet, but I'm sure somebody will see me driving toward my home on Long Island after a ball game and say, "How come you're going this way? Gracie Mansion (the mayor's official residence) is in Manhattan."

Every time I'm up in the clouds, something happens that brings me right back to earth. There was the time a beautiful lady in a white dress drifted across a crowded room just to talk to me. It was the night before the opening of the 1964 Bing Crosby golf tournament at Pebble Beach, California, which I broadcast over NBC. During a glittering cocktail party at the Del Monte Lodge I noticed this stunning woman repeatedly looking in my direction. When she moved toward me I looked to see who the lucky man would be, but there wasn't anyone else that close to me.

When she reached me she said, "I beg your pardon, but I just wanted to tell you that I've seen everything you've ever done on television, and I enjoy it immensely. I just couldn't pass up this chance to talk to you."

I thanked her profusely. She went on to explain that she had come to Pebble Beach with her daughter because they were both golfing addicts, and we discussed the tournament. James Garner, the movie star, who was taking part in the celebrity division, came up and greeted the lady by name.

"Oh, Jim," she said, "you know Chris Schenkel, don't you?"

Schenkel is one of my favorite sports announcers. Curt Gowdy of Boston is another. Both are better-looking than I, as I can prove by the fact that I bear a general resemblance to Warren Spahn. Neither Spahn nor I would ever win a beauty contest. We both have big noses and high foreheads, and we're about the same age.

The first time I was aware anyone had trouble telling us apart was the night before the all-star baseball game in Pittsburgh in 1959. Two fellows stopped me in the lobby of the Carlton House and asked for my autograph. I tried to explain that I wasn't anybody special and that I didn't think they really wanted an autograph from me.

"Oh, but we do, Warren," one said. "We really do."

One night after Spahn joined the Mets for spring training in St. Petersburg, Florida, in 1965, a waiter came up to me at the Wine House in nearby Redington Beach and said, "Please, Warren, may I have your autograph?"

"I'm not Warren Spahn," I said. "I'm just a run-of-the-mill sports broadcaster."

The waiter stared, slightly embarrassed, then said, "Of course. I'm sorry, Curt."

On the way home that spring we played an exhibition game in Portsmouth, Virginia. As we went through the hotel lobby in Norfolk to the bus taking us to the ball park, a woman shoved an autograph book into my hands and said, "Will you sign that please, Mr. Spahn?"

Explaining that I wasn't Spahn, I tried to hand it back, but she wouldn't take it.

"Come on now, don't kid me," she said, following me. "I know you're Warren Spahn."

"But I'm not," I insisted.

She was still with me when I reached the street. Figuring I'd be safe in the bus, I moved faster, but she kept up with me. Hawk Taylor of the Mets hurried by and saw what was happening, so he turned and yelled, "C'mon, Spahnie, the bus is leaving."

"See?" the woman screamed. "You *are* Warren Spahn. Now sign my book."

She followed me right on the bus, still screaming. She didn't shut up until she spotted the real Warren Spahn slumped in an aisle seat. If she hadn't seen him she probably would have clawed me to death. She had her fingernails at the ready.

I traveled around so much with Red Grange during the 1950s that people sometimes got us mixed up. Once, in Iowa City, it happened even after I'd registered at the hotel.

I had never been in Iowa City before. When I checked in, the clerk said, "It's certainly nice to have you back with us again, Mr. Nelson."

I started to correct him, but since he was assigning me my room I didn't want to get into an argument. A bellhop took my bags and as we walked across the lobby to the elevator he said, "It's nice to have you back with us again, Mr. Nelson."

Since I now had my room, I didn't mind arguing with the bellhop, so I said, "But I've never been here before."

"You sure have," he said. "Don't you remember? We put you in the big room on the third floor, and you had the television set."

We spent all the time waiting for the elevator discussing whether I had or hadn't stayed in the hotel, so for the sake of

peace I finally agreed I had. As I came back down on the elevator later, people stared at me, and I heard a woman say, "I've
seen him often on TV."

My chest went out and I glowed with pride. I was the last
one off the elevator. As I stepped out, the operator said, "Nice
to have you back, Mr. Grange."

Down went my chest, and the glow disappeared. "My name
is Nelson," I said.

"Oh," he said. "I thought you were Red Grange. I told that
to the bellhop when you came in, and I saw him run over to tell
the room clerk before you registered. And I've been telling
people in the elevator ever since you got here that Red Grange
is in the house."

I gave up. Even the guys calling me Mr. Nelson thought I
was Red Grange.

Believe it or not, big nose, high forehead, and all, I was once
taken for Ronald Colman, the British movie star. I engineered
that delusion myself. In 1945 I was stuck with the Army in Linz,
Austria, on the banks of the Danube River. World War II had
just ended, and I had enough points to get out, but nobody
was letting me out. We had a baseball league, and I shared the
broadcasting booth with a guy named Charlie Fisher. I guess the
commanding general was so used to our voices he didn't want
to hear anyone else, because he kept telling us what a great job
we were doing.

"We're going to have to do something radical to get out of
here," Fisher said. "Can you talk like Ronald Colman?"

"Can't everybody?" I said.

"Well, practice until you get it down pat. I've got an idea."

I practiced for a couple of weeks, with the barmaids, the
chambermaids, the mermaids, all the maids I met, and pretty
soon I talked so much like Ronald Colman I had trouble talking
like Lindsey Nelson. Charlie's idea was to have a man-in-the-

stands broadcast during a ball game. He would go through the stands interviewing soldiers, and I'd be one of the interviewees.

"Good afternoon, soldier," he said when he came to me. "What's your name?"

"Colman," I mumbled from the depths of my diaphragm. "Private Colman."

"Well, Private Colman," he said, "I didn't know you were with the American Army."

"Oh, yes. I've been with the American Army several months. I'll never forget when I was first assigned to this outfit." I cleared my throat a few times, then grunted, "Quite an outfit! Quite an outfit!"

"Do you like baseball, Private Colman?"

"Indubitably. I shall never forget how I used to race down to the newsstands in London to get the latest American baseball results."

"Thank you, Private Colman," Charlie said. "Thank you very much."

When we got back to the hotel where we were billeted, a staff officer was pacing nervously up and down. He rushed over to us and yelled, "The general wants him transferred to headquarters, and I can't find his name anywhere. What did he look like, Fisher?"

"What did who look like?" Charlie asked.

"You know who I mean. Ronald Colman."

"You mean the guy I interviewed today? Did I say *Ronald* Colman? I thought I said *Private* Colman."

"The general said it was Ronald Colman. He heard him. Now, quick, tell me. What did he look like?"

"Well, let's see," Charlie said, pressing a hand to his head in deep meditation. "He was tall and slender. He was a bit gray about the temples, and he had a little mustache. He wore a summer uniform with a khaki hat cocked on one side of his head."

"Oh, my." The staff officer groaned. "That's him, all right."

They never found Ronald Colman, but they found Charlie and me. We were ordered out of there within a week.

At about nine-thirty one morning ten years later, I was at the corner of Madison Avenue and 46th Street in New York, waiting for a traffic light to change. As I stepped off the curb somebody said, "Ronald Colman, I presume."

It was Charlie Fisher, the only person in the world who thinks of Ronald Colman when he sees me.

In 1964 the Mets had a perfect candidate for confusion in Don Heffner, a coach who later became manager of the Cincinnati Reds. Heffner bears a striking resemblance to Barry Goldwater. A shy, quiet man, he is not particularly at home in crowds, especially when he's the center of attention.

We got into Pittsburgh one day early in the season and were met by the usual collection of youngsters seeking autographs. While waiting for their room assignments, the players obliged in the lobby of the Pittsburgh Hilton, so there was a good deal of activity, as there always is when a big-league ball club arrives in town. It was still going on when the members of a Tuesday sewing club or some such thing got out of lunch. The girls saw the cluster of people in front of the desk and then spotted Heffner.

"There's Goldwater!" one of them shrieked.

The next thing Heffner knew, he was engulfed. Nobody paid any attention to his protests that he was just a baseball coach, not the leading candidate for the Republican nomination for President. It took a flying wedge of bellhops and ballplayers to get him to an elevator.

"It's going to be a rough season," he remarked later.

It was. He had to learn to walk with his head down and sneak through lobbies like a thief in the night to keep from getting mobbed.

Banquet-hopping is part of every baseball broadcaster's winter schedule. An announcer could be out every night if he weren't careful, because he's usually the first guy people think of for the job of toastmaster at any sports function. I don't mind banquets as long as I can space them far enough apart. They've given me some of the best laughs of my career.

One night in February of 1964 I went to Auburn, New York, for a sports banquet, along with Tom Meany, umpire Tom Gorman, Wid Matthews of the Mets front office, Tracy Stallard of the Mets, and Jim Bouton of the Yankees. As we sat down at the head table I was pleased to see there were plenty of speakers, since that meant no one man would have to talk too long. During dessert, people came up with programs to be autographed. I had signed half a dozen when a youngster passed me one folded open. To my amazement, there was a full-page picture of me on that page.

Before I could say anything, the master of ceremonies, who was sitting beside me, leaned over and said, "Oh, Lindsey, we forgot to tell you. You're the principal speaker tonight."

Surprises like that don't come very often, but with the Mets you never know. The night before the 1965 baseball season opened there was a mammoth welcome-home dinner for the ball club at the New York Hilton. I hadn't been directly invited, but learned second-hand that Ralph Kiner, Bob Murphy, and I were expected there to help introduce the players. None of us would have missed the affair anyhow.

I took my time driving into town. The ballroom was jammed and, since I didn't have a ticket, I had to check in at the door. Arthur Richman, the Mets promotion man, pulled me aside and said, "Will you introduce Jane Jarvis at the organ when she plays the national anthem?"

I said sure, figuring this was a little added job. But after I got inside somebody said, "Lindsey, I'd like to go over these cards with you."

The cards were the names of speakers and ballplayers to

introduce. When we reached the fifth or sixth one, a light suddenly dawned.

"Wait a minute," I said. "What do I have to do with these cards?"

"Didn't anybody tell you?" came the reply. "You're the master-of-ceremonies tonight."

A few years ago I went to an alumni gathering at a church school with my wife, Mickie, at the invitation of one of the officials she knew. She sat on one side of the master-of-ceremonies, with me on the other. The talk was a little strained, because nobody at the head table seemed to know anybody else. Finally the M.C. turned to Mickie and said, "You must get a big thrill every morning, picking up the paper and seeing your husband's picture at the top of his column." She did a double take, and so did I. The man excused himself went over to talk to somebody else, and came back armed with the knowledge that I was an announcer, not a newspaper columnist. A good thing, too, since he had the job of introducing me.

Red Grange and I once walked into the Driskill Hotel in Austin for a game the next day. There was a big placard in the lobby reading: "Sports dinner, six-thirty tonight. Hear Red Grange and Lindsey Nelson."

"Do you know anything about it?" I asked.

"Nope," he said. "Do you?"

"Nope."

Later in the day we were watching television. At the station break there was a picture of the two of us together, with the notation: "Sports dinner, Driskill Hotel, six-thirty tonight. Hear Red Grange and Lindsey Nelson."

Again we assured each other that we knew nothing about the affair. About an hour later the phone rang, and the caller said, "Wonder if you and Red would mind dropping by tonight. We're having a sports dinner."

"Six-thirty at the Driskill," I said. "We'll be there."

I was in the Mets broadcasting booth at Al Lang Field in St. Petersburg one day in the spring of 1965 when a stranger stopped in and identified himself as a member of the committee in charge of the annual Governor's Dinner in Tampa. I had already agreed to act as M.C. This man just wanted to tell me what time to be at the Tampa Terrace Hotel and where to go after I arrived.

When I appeared in the room at the appointed time, I was met by another member of the committee. We introduced ourselves and were chatting when the guy who had approached me at the ball park walked in. He nodded when I spoke to him, then, looking preoccupied and a little harassed, he walked around the room a couple of times and finally said he had to get back to the banquet hall. At the door he turned and said to the other man, "When Lindsey Nelson shows up, tell him I'm downstairs."

He was ten feet down the corridor before we could stop him.

That was the dinner at which I read the doggerel verse, including my deathless lines about Judge Roy Hofheinz and the Astrodome. I did something else at that dinner I had never tried before. I told a couple of Casey Stengel stories in Stengelese with Casey in the audience. I had done it often without him, but this was the first time he had ever seen me mimic him.

I was a little concerned how he would take it, especially after a terrific burst of applause when I finished the second story. Casey was at a table in the back of the hall, and I hardly dared look at him. But, great showman that he is, he stood up and took a deep bow while the hundreds of baseball men present clapped and cheered.

Later he came around back of the dais, stuck out his hand as he passed me, and said, "You done splendid."

That was the supreme accolade.

Chapter 3

The
Fabulous
Liberty
Network

THE Mets set up their first ticket office in November of 1961 at the Martinique Hotel, about seven blocks south of the Metropolitan Opera House in Manhattan. Bill Gibson, who had run the old Brooklyn Dodgers ticket office at Ebbets Field, was in charge. He put up only one small sign. It read: METS TICKET OFFICE.

The Mets were new, and the Martinique was just close enough to the opera house to invite confusion. Inevitably, somebody stepped up to Gibson's booth one day and said, "I'd like two for *Traviata.*"

"Where would you like them?" Bill asked. "On the first- or the third-base side?"

My first real training for the Mets announcing job came when I went to Dallas to join Gordon McLendon's Liberty

Broadcasting System as an announcer in 1951. McLendon, an ardent sports fan who couldn't get a job with any of the existing radio networks after World War II, solved the problem by starting his own. With a minimum of cash and a maximum of nerve, ingenuity, enterprise, and imagination, Gordon ran his Liberty network up to a fantastic 431 stations before it collapsed about a year after I arrived on the scene.

The foundation of the Liberty network was built on a system of broadcasting ball games known as re-creations. This was handled by an announcer in a studio, relaying telegraphic reports to his own audience over the air. The reports, direct from the ball park where the game was being played, consisted of the barest information transmitted in a simple code which any baseball fan could easily interpret.

For example, "B1" meant "ball one," "S1–C" meant "strike one called," "F1" meant "Foul," and so on. The positions were numbered by standard scoring procedure, with the pitcher 1, the catcher 2, the first baseman 3, the second baseman 4, the third baseman 5, the shortstop 6, the left fielder 7, the center fielder 8, and the right fielder 9. Thus, "4–3" on the wire meant that the batter was out, second baseman to first baseman. Or "F–9" meant the batter flied out to the right fielder.

In those days Western Union would furnish a telegraphic description of any major league baseball game for a flat rate of $27.50, as long as you had permission of the home team. This was more or less automatic. Ball clubs were delighted to get their games into far-off communities. It was good publicity not only for the team but for its city, and it certainly wouldn't hurt the attendance.

McLendon sold his re-creations for something like ten dollars a game, with the station also paying its own telephone-line charges. The more stations, the lower the line charges for any individual station, because it had to pay the charges only to the nearest city already getting the re-creations, which in turn paid only to *its* nearest city.

This was the first time major-league baseball on a day-to-day basis had ever been available by radio to cities off the big-league beaten path. None of the franchises had yet been moved, so the big leagues were still confined to the northeastern part of the country. All the rest was wide open. McLendon simply moved in and took over the West Coast, the Southwest, and the South, where he and his network soon became better known among sports fans than far more famous announcers and far more solid networks.

When I was with NBC after Liberty folded, I tried to rent a car in Los Angeles but had trouble establishing my credit. I showed them my NBC card and various other forms of identification, but the clerk wasn't satisfied. As he watched me flip through my wallet, he spotted an old Liberty card I still carried.

"Wait a minute," he said. "Liberty Broadcasting System. Of course! I've heard you do hundreds of baseball games. What kind of a car do you want?"

The first time I went to San Francisco to do a football game for NBC, a sports writer remarked, "How come an old baseball broadcaster like you is doing a football game?" All he had ever heard me do were baseball games over Liberty.

I was reminded of that incident when, after I started broadcasting Met games, people often came up and said, "What's an old football man like you doing on a baseball broadcast?" Since the Liberty network never reached any big-league cities, they thought baseball announcing was new to me.

McLendon became popular by the original manner in which he and his staff re-created games. Some announcers around the country played them straight, simply repeating to their audiences the bare facts that came over the telegraphic wires. This, of course, resulted in dull presentations with long gaps between pitches or plays. The better announcers filled the gaps with comment about the game and the players, and other bits of information.

Gordon went farther. By using all sorts of mechanical devices, he made a re-creation sound as if the game were being broadcast direct from the ball park. He got so excited—and demanded the same excitement from his announcers—that Liberty's re-creations were often more interesting than broadcasts direct from the scene.

There were always four turntables of recordings going in the studio, two with general crowd noise and two with excited crowd noise. The audio engineer would fade this in to fit the narration. The announcer wore a head set so he could hear the crowd, which had an amazing effect on him. As the crowd got excited, he got excited. His voice rose automatically, and he would transmit his own excitement to the audience. Sometimes the engineer would beef up the crowd noise even if nothing happened on the field to justify it. The announcer then had to invent a reason—perhaps a spectator making a sensational catch of a foul ball into the stands, or a peanut vendor falling downstairs, or a couple of guys getting into a fight.

In the interest of accuracy, McLendon sent an engineer to every ball park in the big leagues to tape the playing of the national anthem and other local music, as well as crowd sounds. When, for example, somebody yelled above the crowd at Fenway Park, it was in a Boston accent and would be used in a Red Sox re-creation. When a Liberty announcer told his audience that Gladys Goodding would play "The Star-Spangled Banner" on the organ from Ebbets Field in Brooklyn, listeners actually heard organ music played by Gladys Goodding from Ebbets Field.

By the time I joined the network Liberty was broadcasting both live and by re-creation, often doing one game in the daytime and the other at night. I once did sixty games in a single

month, which wasn't unusual. Everybody else did it at one time
or another.

We used Gene Mack's famous cartoon drawings of the
big-league ball parks to describe these places accurately in
re-creations. The drawings also came in handy for the re-creation
of old-time games, an invention of McLendon's which was a
sure-fire hit everywhere. Mack pinpointed exactly where famous
plays took place, and we would describe them in the course of
doing a World Series game of half a century ago. We went all
the way back to the play-by-play of 1869 Cincinnati Red Stock-
ing games, drawing generously on our imaginations. More than
once I had time called while the ball was being retrieved from
under the hoofs of a horse attached to a carriage parked along
one of the foul lines.

When McLendon began re-creating old-time games, he referred to himself as "the Old Scotchman" to suggest a character
of such ancient vintage he could recall the incidents from personal memory. At the time Gordon himself was not yet thirty,
but millions of listeners pictured him as a very old man. Even
when broadcasting a modern game, Gordon identified himself
as "the Old Scotchman."

He did the famous games of baseball history, including
Merkle's bonehead of 1908, the game in which Ty Cobb slashed
Home Run Baker in 1909, and the twenty-six-inning game of
1920, in which Leon Cadore of the Dodgers and Joe Oeschger
of the Braves went the entire distance in a historic 1–1 deadlock. We all did these old games at one time or another, but
only Gordon was "the Old Scotchman." The rest of us were
ourselves.

The Liberty Broadcasting System grew and grew and grew,
until it was exceeded only by Mutual in the number of affiliated
stations. By then we used station breaks identifying ourselves—
with perfect accuracy—as "America's second largest network."

It was a peculiar period in the broadcasting industry. Television was still in its infancy, but everyone recognized it as the coming giant, and the big networks weren't paying much attention to radio, which they thought was dying. Their heaviest concentration was on television.

But there were vast areas of the country which weren't yet interconnected and couldn't get television live. Only kinescoped television reached these areas. It was sometimes as much as a week old, nothing more than a novelty for those who could afford TV sets. And in those sections of the country radio was still very much alive, as Gordon McLendon well knew.

It was in this atmosphere that the Liberty Broadcasting Company, the brainchild of one imaginative idea man, flourished. McLendon built it up into a fantastic news operation that included some of radio's biggest names, such people as William L. Shirer, Raymond Gram Swing, Joseph C. Harsch, and Westbrook Van Voorhies. At one point Mickey Rooney did a daily sports show for LBS. Besides the Dallas building, the network had offices and studios on Madison Avenue in New York and in Hollywood, California.

In accordance with FCC regulations, we always announced before and after a game that it was a re-creation and not live, but this didn't mean anything to the audience. Everything sounded so realistic that people forgot the announcer was in a studio in Dallas instead of on the scene. Besides, so many broadcasts actually were live that I'm sure most listeners assumed they all were.

We used every device we could to make them think so. One day while I was re-creating a game from Griffith Stadium in Washington, McLendon dropped by the studio, so I said, "Coming into our booth right now is the president of the Liberty Broadcasting System, Gordon McLendon."

Gordon leaned over and said into the microphone, "Ah, yes, Washington, D.C. And at this time of the year the cherry blossoms are beautiful."

He didn't say we were in Washington, only that the cherry blossoms there were beautiful, which, of course, they are. And he was careful not to use the words "here" or "there." At Liberty these were poisonous during re-creations. "Here" would have been a direct lie and "there" a dead giveaway.

In order to enhance the re-creations, McLendon assigned somebody each day to act as the public-address announcer at the ball park. When there was a substitution or a change of pitchers or a pinch-hitter, this announcer talked in the background, so that to listeners he sounded as if he were right at the field. This required an echo effect. One of Gordon's engineers decided the best place for this was the men's room, which was small and handy to the studio. Whenever we did a re-creation the men's room was closed to everyone but the "PA announcer." He would sit in the studio with whoever was broadcasting the game, watching the telegraphic ticker for his cue to go to his post. When he got there, the broadcaster would say, "There's a new pitcher coming in, but we'll wait for the announcement."

From the men's room would come a muffled bellow, "Smith, number twenty-seven, now pitching for Chicago." The man at the microphone would then say, "We have it now. Smith, number twenty-seven, is in to pitch for the White Sox."

When I first joined Liberty I re-created a game out of Pittsburgh. Billy Meyer was then the Pirates manager. Meyer's home town was Knoxville, where I had been broadcasting and working as sports publicity director at the University of Tennessee before going to Dallas. The Knoxville newspapers requested a picture of Meyer and me together in Pittsburgh. Billy was there all right, but I was nowhere near the place. They had to settle for pictures of us individually.

McLendon had begun his network in a basement studio at the Cliff Towers Hotel in Oak Cliff, across the river from Dallas. By the time I started working for him—for $125 a week—he had built a two-story building at 2100 Jackson Street downtown. Its most impressive feature was a huge map of the United States on the lobby wall, with the cities linked together by lines criss-crossing each other. I made the same mistake everyone else did. I assumed it was a map of the Liberty network. Actually, it was an American Airlines map.

The first person Gordon introduced me to was John Kieran, Jr., son of the author and former *New York Times* sports columnist. Johnny, who had been a classmate of Gordon's at Yale, was his culture man. His title was assistant to the president, but his principal job was to turn out epigrams for use in the appropriate places on the air. We all had instructions to fit them in wherever we could. Gordon had two favorites. At the bottom half of the first inning he would say, "It's the home half of the hello frame." And when the home team came up in the last of the ninth four or five runs behind, he proclaimed that "the prospects are as black as the inside of a cat."

McLendon waxed so lyrical in his baseball broadcasts that some of his listeners never forgot the deathless prose with which Kieran provided him. Some years later Willie Morris, in a *New Yorker* piece, referred to McLendon as "the best rhetorician outside of Nye Bevan and Theodore Bilbo I have ever heard." Wrote Morris:

Under his handling, a baseball game took on a life of its own. His games were rare and remarkable entities, things of beauty. Casual pop flies had the flow of history behind them, double plays resembled the stark, tragic clashes of old armies, and home runs deserved acknowledgment on Grecian urns. Later when I came across Thomas Wolfe, I felt I had heard him before, from Shibe Park, Crosley Field, and Yankee Stadium. On those summer afternoons, almost every radio in town was tuned to the Old Scotchman, and his rhetoric dominated the place; it hovered in the branches of the trees, bounced off the hills, and came out of car exhausts . . . from then on, accurate, up-to-the-minute baseball news was disreputable in the town. I believe we all went back to the Scotchman not merely out of loyalty but because he touched our need for a simple and unmitigated eloquence. In Mississippi, I sometimes think now, it was the final flowering of a poetic age.

On my first day at work, both McLendon and Kieran told me to wander around and make myself at home. "I want you just to get familiar with the operation for a few days," Gordon said. "You can go on the air after you get the hang of things around here."

That afternoon I opened a door and found McLendon sitting on a bar stool looking over the shoulder of a telegraph operator and re-creating a ball game. Kieran was at a typewriter nearby. When I appeared, McLendon announced, "And now, coming in to do the play-by-play, the new voice of the Liberty Broadcasting System, Lindsey Nelson." Then he and Kieran got up and walked out.

I didn't know the score, the inning, or even who was playing. All I could do was slide onto the stool and see what the operator, a wonderful guy named Jack Marshall, was typing. An old McLendon hand, he recognized my predicament instantly and wrote something like, "Reds leading, 4–1, Blackwell pitching, Bell up for Pirates, one out, nobody on, last of fifth." By having Blackwell paw the earth around the pitcher's mound, reach for the rosin bag, lean forward for the sign, and nod his head, I managed to stall long enough to get organized.

The only times we were ever in real trouble with re-creations were when the telegraph line went dead. When this happened to me one day, I made the pitcher sound slower than cold molasses. The best stalling device was to have him bend down and tie his shoelace. This guy couldn't get his tied at all. He kept straightening up, looking for the sign, throwing to first base to hold the runner on, kicking the rubber, going to the rosin bag—and bending down to tie his shoelace.

Finally I just had to start the ball game again, so I had him throw ball one. I continued to stall, hoping the wire would come alive, and finally ran the count to three balls and two strikes. Then I used foul balls until they were sprayed all over the park. I had the batter hitting about fifteen fouls and the pitcher endlessly stopping to tie his shoelaces before the ticker started clattering again.

"Runner out stealing, 2–4," came the message.

Action at last! I was overjoyed.

"Now," I said, "the runner at first takes his lead, the pitcher is up and set. He stretches, checks the runner . . . here's the pitch . . . it's outside . . . the runner's going . . . the catcher throws . . . he's out!"

Only then did I realize that I had thrown a baserunner out at second on a base on balls to the batter. Even the Mets never did that. I was ten years ahead of my time.

Sometimes Liberty was even ahead of the ball game. The Mutual Broadcasting System did certain big-league ball games live, so there were competitive broadcasts in many cities around the country if we happened to be re-creating the same game. Fans often switched their dials back and forth to make comparisons. When the game was dull or the live crowd apathetic, Mutual suffered. They couldn't make excitement where there wasn't any, but we could. They couldn't anticipate what might happen, either, but we weren't afraid to anticipate anything that seemed logical.

One day I was re-creating a game that Mutual was doing live when the batter came up in a late inning with his team three runs behind. The count went to three balls and no strikes. Everybody knew he would take the next pitch, and it was a fairly good bet that the pitcher would get it over the plate. "The next pitch is in there for a called strike," I said.

Mutual hadn't reported it because it hadn't happened yet. Fortunately for us, it did happen. Twenty minutes later the Mutual announcer, whom we were monitoring, said on the air, "We just got a telegram saying, 'Why can't you keep up with the Liberty Broadcasting System?' We're here and they're not, so I don't see how we could be behind them."

We did almost as many games live as we re-created. McLendon, with his colossal nerve and friendly charm, had long ago obtained permission to put our telephone lines into most of the major-league parks. Later, probably on the theory that McLendon would do the games anyhow, every major-league team except the St. Louis Cardinals granted him broadcasting rights to any game on the regular season's schedule. I'm not sure why the Cardinals refused; this happened before I went to work for Liberty. It had something to do with their own network, which was the biggest in the majors and spread to so many places south and west of St. Louis that it competed with ours.

Since he loved both baseball and travel, McLendon personally did as many games live as he could. The 1951 National League race was a frenetic stretch run between the Brooklyn Dodgers and the New York Giants. Gordon was on the road with one team or the other for most of the month of September, and we re-created whatever other games had any bearing on the race.

The Giants closed the season in Boston, and the Dodgers in Philadelphia, on a Sunday afternoon. McLendon decided to do the Giants game live and arrange to have the Dodgers play-by-play sent to us in Dallas. Naturally, we couldn't do both games at once, but if the Dodgers game continued after the Giants game ended we would start re-creating it when Gordon went off the air.

Our big competition that day was Mutual, which also did the Giants game live. When the Giants won in Boston, that ended Mutual's baseball play-by-play, but we picked up the Dodgers game, which lasted fourteen innings. Although a re-creation, the broadcast sounded live, and I'm sure most of our listeners thought it was.

The season ended in a tie, so Gordon went to New York to do the three-game playoff between the Giants and the Dodgers. The first game was in Brooklyn, with the next two in New York. Without bothering to check with anybody for permission, although these games were not part of the regular season's schedule, Gordon simply went in and broadcast them. The Giants won the first game, and the Dodgers the second, so the playoff went down to one grand finale in the Polo Grounds.

As soon as the second game ended we had a telephone call in Dallas from a New York advertising agency, asking if we would be interested in buying the broadcast rights to the third. Obviously the caller didn't know that we had already done the first two. We decided the best thing to do was stall him off. We told him we'd let him know, and then we closed the switchboard.

It stayed closed for the next twenty-four hours. The Liberty Broadcasting System didn't reopen for business until that third playoff game was over. That was the day of Bobby Thomson's historic game-winning home run which won the pennant for the Giants. With no phones to answer and no re-creations to make, we all sat entranced as we listened to it at the studio in Dallas. It was one of the most dramatic sports broadcasts I have ever heard. Gordon's opening line was something like, "From the Bay of Tokyo to the tip of Land's End . . . *this* is the day." From then on he pulled out all the stops, and that, I'm sure, was the high point of his announcing career. It was also the high point of the network's.

That fall Gordon made me director of football, which meant I would be in charge of scheduling games, negotiating for rights, and doing much of the announcing. It did not mean a raise in salary. In the absence of ready cash, we dealt heavily in titles, which were frequently changed. Every new title was announced as a promotion. The newspapers around the country cooperated beautifully. What we didn't get in money was made up for in prestige and national publicity.

We had a heavy football schedule. On Friday nights we broadcast University of Miami games; on Saturday afternoon, Eastern college games followed by West Coast college games; on Saturday nights, Louisiana State games; and on Sundays, two National Football League games, one from New York, the other from Los Angeles.

Obviously I had to do a lot of traveling. I cut the schedule so thin that I never knew whether I'd make a game on time or not. I warned Gordon about this, but he pooh-poohed the possibility of my getting hung up somewhere when I was supposed to be somewhere else. He didn't know where I was most of the time anyhow.

"One of these days," I told him, "I'll be stuck in Peoria with a game to do in Oklahoma City."

"It'll never happen," he said.

Oddly enough, it never did, although I came close a few times.

One day Gordon told me to negotiate for the rights to the Senior Bowl game, which then was carried by CBS, so I set up a meeting in New York with the Senior Bowl general manager, Ray Schuessler. The only time we could make it was Sunday morning. I was doing the Tennessee–Mississippi game at Oxford, Mississippi, Saturday afternoon, and the Cleveland Browns–New York Giants game at the Polo Grounds Sunday.

I flew to Memphis, where I rented a car and drove to Oxford. There was a flight out of Memphis for New York which I could just about make if the game didn't take too long, but it was touch and go. On the road back to Memphis the car suddenly coughed and died on me. I grabbed my bag and typewriter and started hitchhiking. A pickup truck took me to the outskirts of Memphis; from there I got a cab to the airport.

My plane was long gone, but there was a flight to St. Louis with a close connection to a New York flight. I made it by a hair and arrived in New York, tired but triumphant, early Sunday morning.

Schuessler came over to see me at the hotel. After he left I called McLendon in Dallas.

"Hello, Lindsey," he said. "Where are you, boy?"

"I'm in New York."

"Do we have something in New York today?"

"The Giants and the Browns."

"Great," he said. "I'll be listening."

"I almost didn't get here," I said. "My car broke down outside of Oxford."

There was a pause. Then Gordon said, "Well, you're there, aren't you?"

"Barely."

"Then what are you worried about?" he asked.

The first time I broadcast a football game at Wrigley Field in Chicago I couldn't get in through the press gate because I had no ticket, so I went in with the peanut vendors and the sweepers at the employees' entrance. After locating our radio booth, I bought a program and a hot dog and sat down to wait for the engineer to set up the amplifier and the lines.

He got caught in traffic and didn't arrive until minutes before the game began. Thirty seconds before kickoff we finally were on the air with our opening slogan: "Play ball with the Liberty Broadcasting System!"

When I got back to Dallas, Gordon said, "That was a fine broadcast, Lindsey."

"Thanks," I said. "Only I almost didn't make it. I had to sneak into the ball park, and the engineer was so late we nearly missed the boat. It seems to me we ought to plan things a little better."

"No, it was just great," Gordon said. "I was completely satisfied."

Everything was just great with Gordon, and that was the trouble. While it was a delight to work for him, his casual optimism led to the undoing of the whole network. He trusted everyone, a dangerous thing to do when you're dealing with 431 affiliates all over the United States. We did everything on credit, with the result that we actually operated almost continuously on a cash shoestring.

The straw that broke the camel's back was the loss of our baseball sponsor, the Falstaff Brewing Company, because of a disagreement on price. They switched over to Mutual for the 1952 season, and that was the beginning of the end for us. An added problem was the increasing difficulty in purchasing broadcasting rights. The ball clubs weren't so willing to let us in any more.

One day I ran into one of the Liberty vice presidents on the street in Dallas. He had just come from a meeting with McLendon and other officials and looked as if he had lost his last friend.

"Lindsey," he said, putting his arm around me, "if you were in a building that started collapsing around your ears, what would you do?"

"I'd get out," I said.

"Well," he said, "what are you waiting for?"

I resigned the next morning.

Chapter 4

"Wot
Ees
Thees
'Uddle?"

THE St. Louis Cardinals were hailed as the baseball champions of the world in 1964 because they beat the Yankees in an October series. Met fans know better. The Mets went to St. Louis on October 1 that year and beat the Cardinals two games out of three. Since they were the only team to win an October series with the Cardinals, who then went on to beat the Yankees, that made the Mets the baseball champions of 1964, didn't it? Naturally.

Gordon McLendon asked me to stick around a couple of weeks, so of course I did. Liberty was obviously on its last legs, and everybody was looking around for jobs. An old friend of mine, Cecil Beaver, who owned station WHHM in Memphis, asked me to go there to re-create big-league games for him. He had a sponsor for the broadcasts he had been getting from

Liberty and wanted to save the account after the network folded. I agreed to go on a temporary basis, with the understanding that I would move on when something better turned up.

Something better was already in the works, thanks to Matty Brescia, Liberty's publicity director. He was phoning friends in the broadcasting business all over the country in search of a job for me. One day, just before I left Dallas, I got a call from Tom Gallery, the new sports director of NBC. Brescia knew him, but I had never met him.

"How would you like to be assistant director of sports for the NBC radio and television networks?" he asked.

It took two months for the job to develop. While waiting, I had an offer to do Cleveland Browns football games. I went to Cleveland to see Hamilton Shea of Station WTAM, and Paul Brown, the Browns coach. In those days Brown was practically the ball club. He made all the decisions both on and off the field, and he apparently was going to make this one. He quizzed me all morning, asking searching questions as he put me through a thorough examination of my knowledge of football and the people in it.

Just before we left he said, "When Mrs. Brown and I go out socially we wouldn't think of calling on anybody not directly connected with the ball club. We build our social life within its structure, and we would expect you to do the same."

I didn't have to worry about my social life in Cleveland. WTAM was an NBC affiliate, and Tom Gallery knew I had been offered the job there. I was sitting in Tom's office in New York a few days after my visit to Cleveland when Gallery phoned Ham Shea in my presence.

"We've just decided that Lindsey will stay here," he said. "Thanks very much for waiting." After hanging up, he shook hands and said, "Welcome aboard." That's how I learned I had the NBC job.

Before starting back to Memphis to get my affairs there

settled, I called my wife, who was in our home town of Columbia, Tennessee, waiting to find out where we were going.

"We're going to New York," I told her.

"Fine," she said. "What kind of a job is it?"

"A good one. Assistant director of sports for NBC radio and
television."

"How much will you make?"

I paused. Then I said, "Y'know, honey, I haven't the slightest
idea."

Gallery and I had never discussed my salary. I didn't know
what it was until I got my first check. Before that came, I had
to have money to move. I asked Tom if the network might help
me with expenses.

"How much do you need?" he asked.

"About three hundred and fifty," I said.

"Well," he said, "we can't pay your moving expenses. Tell
you what, though. The Bill Stern show Friday night is running
about twenty seconds short. Could you do those twenty
seconds?"

"Sure."

"Good. We'll give you a talent fee of three hundred and fifty."

"Tom," I said, "this is my kind of business."

Gallery was a fantastic guy in a fantastic profession. A bluff,
friendly Irishman with an almost perpetual grin on his face, he
was a former movie actor who once played second fiddle to a
dog. In the Rin-Tin-Tin pictures of the twenties, Tom had been
the male lead. The pay was good, but the job frustrating. Everybody was so busy kowtowing to the dog that nobody worried
about the man.

The payoff came when Tom, playing the part of a young flyer
forced down in flames, was being rescued by Rin-Tin-Tin. Tom
was wearing a shoulder harness with a leather thong that came
out of his shirt collar at the back of his neck. The dog was supposed to rush into the flames and pull him out by the thong,

but instead grabbed him by one ear. Unable to wriggle loose, Tom finally kicked Rin-Tin-Tin in the chops, to the horror of everyone from the director to the trainer. Things were never quite the same after that.

In those days Gallery was very much a part of the Hollywood scene. He knew all the old-time movie stars. He drove a yellow custom-built convertible so slick that Red Grange asked for one just like it before signing a movie contract in 1926. Gallery, Grange, Adolph Menjou, Johnny Mack Brown, and several others were members of a rotating poker game that had been going on before Gallery got into the movies and was still going after he got out.

Sports interested Tom more than movies, and he began promoting fights at the Hollywood Legion Stadium. He made Friday fight night in Hollywood, with all the stars, semi-stars, and would-be stars in regular attendance. He promoted the Joe Louis–Jack Roper heavyweight championship fight there, with Bing Crosby doing the color commentary on radio. He promoted other sports events there too, then became general manager of the Brooklyn Dodgers pro football team owned by Dan Topping. From there he went to the Yankees, to the Dumont Television Network, and finally to NBC.

It was Gallery who introduced me to the advertising battleground of Madison Avenue, a strange and wonderful world which never ceases to fascinate me. One day I went to a meeting with Tom, Russ Hodges, and Mike Dann. Hodges, one of my favorite characters, was the New York Giants announcer and still does the Giants games in San Francisco. Dann, later a CBS vice president in charge of programing, was then a sports salesman for NBC.

We were ushered into a conference room filled with people none of us had ever met before. Our account man introduced Dann, who began pitching a new sports show, the details of which I'm sure he was making up as he went along.

"This show," he said, "will be by far the most important segment of our entire over-all afternoon of football programing."

He looked around the room. Everyone was smiling expectantly.

"While we will be presenting a pre-game show that will point up the game that we will be covering play-by-play," he went on, "and we will be presenting the game-of-the-week itself, which will be of great interest to football fans all across the country, this show, which will follow the game, will capture the interest of *all* the fans because it will feature scores of *all* the games."

A master! Just clear enough to give the idea, just muddy enough to confuse. What a salesman! He covered the show in intimate detail, playing those faces around the table as if they were a fine instrument. If there were frowns, he changed the tune. If smiles, he increased the volume.

A portly, distinguished gentleman appeared at the door and looked around. Mike, right in the middle of a sentence, motioned him to a vacant chair and, as the man slid into it, went on with his pitch.

"Of course," he said, "we will not depend entirely on just scores to hold the interest of fans, because we will integrate audio feeds into the format of the show from time to time, and the audio feed will supplement the video presentation of the final results with detail of the highlights. The combination will be enough to satisfy the appetite of the most voracious football fan."

Now Mike was staring at the newcomer, who seemed enthralled. He continued talking, raising and lowering his voice to suit the mood of the room. Finally he said, "We will have Joe Hasel stationed at one of the outstanding games other than the one we're covering on game-of-the-week, and we will also have other top-flight football announcers available, with Russ Hodges the anchor man for the whole presentation at the studio here."

Mike looked around the room, turned toward the newcomer, and asked, "Any questions?"

"Yes," the man said. "Is this the Lady Esther conference?"

Out on the street we all congratulated Mike on a fine presentation. He thanked us, then asked me what I thought of it.

"Great," I said. "Only there was one thing I didn't understand. What's an audio feed?"

He grinned. "Simplest thing in the world," he said. "An audio feed is a phone call."

I hadn't come so far from the Liberty Broadcasting System after all.

While life at NBC was nowhere nearly so frenetic as life with Gordon McLendon, we had our share of laughs. In 1954 I went to Montreal with Sleepy Jim Crowley, one of Notre Dame's famed Four Horsemen, to do a Canadian football game-of-the-week. The television crew was mostly French-speaking and with little knowledge of football. To familiarize them with the problems, we had a "dress rehearsal," an exhibition game a few days before the one we were to telecast. For this purpose I had a headset and a direct line to the control truck.

After the first play, the camera swung up into the stands for a crowd shot.

"Get on the huddle," I whispered.

The crew paid no attention. The camera didn't go back to the field until the next play. After that was over, it swung back to the crowd again.

"Hey, get on the huddle," I said.

They still paid no attention. When this happened a third time, I yelled, "The huddle, the huddle—get the camera on the huddle!"

That time I heard a thin, heavily accented voice through the headset, asking, "Wot ees thees 'uddle?"

I worked for three years with Leo Durocher on the baseball game-of-the-week, and we never had a cross word or even a mild misunderstanding. Although he too was then under contract to NBC, I hadn't known him well because he spent most of his time on the West Coast. When we were named to do the game-of-the-week in 1957, I phoned him and we agreed to meet in San Antonio, Texas, to watch the Braves and the Dodgers in an exhibition game. We would then go to Dallas the next day and do a telecast of another exhibition game between the two teams.

As we started into the ball park in San Antonio, Leo said, "Look, Lindsey, I've been in the major leagues thirty-five years, and I think I know something about baseball. But I don't know a thing about television. You tell me what to do, and I'll do it."

Durocher did a great job for us, although he had a habit, which he never overcame, of anticipating plays. I'll never forget his first play-by-play broadcast. It was a game involving Pittsburgh. When I turned the microphone over to Leo, the Pirates were three runs behind, with a runner on first and nobody out. Here is what he said:

"The Pirates have a man on first, nobody out, three runs behind, so the runner won't be going . . . no need to take a chance three runs behind . . . he'll be staying close to the bag— By God, there he goes!"

I think any experienced sportscaster will tell you that the toughest sport to cover is golf. You never know which player to follow. Too many have a chance to win, and you'd probably pick the wrong man. Even if you had the right one, you couldn't keep up with him, as the players move over a vast area and you'd be stuck up on a platform somewhere. The only perfect way to cover golf would be to have an entire crew at each hole, and the cost of that would be prohibitive. Refinements have improved golf coverage tremendously, but when we started coast-to-coast telecasting we had to use a trial-and-error method that was more error than trial.

The first full network telecast of a golf tournament was the 1954 National Open, at Baltusrol in New Jersey, which I did with Craig Wood, a former Open champion. We stationed

ourselves on the roof of the clubhouse, from where we had a
fine view of the eighteenth green, but not of the eighteenth
fairway. There were two cameras behind the green, looking
right down the fairway, and a Cadillac mobile unit was supposed
to follow any player from tee to green. This was the same unit
NBC had used to cover the Inaugural parade in January of 1953.

Driving a mobile unit down Pennsylvania Avenue in Washington is one thing, but driving it along a bumpy golf fairway
is quite another. We soon abandoned that idea and concen-
trated on getting whatever we could from the cameras at the
eighteenth green. That taught us another lesson: don't ever put
an announcer where he doesn't have an even break with the
cameras. The fact that the cameras could see more than we
could put us in a terrible mess.

We had a monitor, but in those days technicians didn't know
much about shading monitors. In the bright sunlight, ours was
washed out completely. We knew Lloyd Mangrum and Gene
Littler were coming down the eighteenth fairway, but all we
could see on the monitor was a couple of dim figures. We both
knelt down and tried to shade the set, but that didn't help. The
camera started closing in on one of the golfers, so in desperation
we just had to guess who it was—and we guessed wrong. Millions
of watchers could clearly see how wrong we were. For the next
month NBC was flooded with letters from fans demanding why
they used announcers who couldn't tell Mangrum from Littler.

The first hour of this telecast was sustaining, and the second
sponsored by Kelly-Springfield Tires. At the end of the sustaining hour, we had a station break, then started the second hour
with a commercial. The concept made sense and everything
went off very nicely, except that, while the commercial was on,
Ed Furgol won the Open. He holed out during the station
break, and we got back just in time to catch him signing his
card while everyone crowded around to congratulate him.

The Open was at San Francisco the next year, and that time

I worked with Gene Sarazen, one of the immortals of the game. Soon after we began the telecast, Ben Hogan came in with what appeared to be the lowest score, which would make him the first man ever to win the Open five times. Sarazen rushed down to congratulate him, and for the rest of the hour we were on we kept talking about Hogan as the probable winner.

But Mark Cox, a Chicago sports fan who was helping us out during the telecast, noticed that Hogan wasn't quite home free.

"There's a guy with a chance to catch him," Mark said just before we went off the air.

"Who?" I asked.

"Jack Fleck," he said.

"Who's Jack Fleck?" I said.

Mark looked him up and learned that he was a club professional from Davenport, Iowa, who had never finished high in a PGA tournament. I did have the wit to mention before we signed off that this complete unknown was the only player in the tournament with a chance to tie Hogan. Sure enough, he did—ten minutes after our coverage of the tournament ended. The next day he won the championship in a playoff. At least that time we had protected ourselves, thanks to Mark Cox. If he hadn't noticed that Fleck had a chance, we probably would have proclaimed Hogan champion before he had won.

In my years at NBC I covered all manner of major sports: in golf, the Open, the Masters, the Las Vegas Tournament of Champions, the Goodall Round Robin, the Tam o' Shanter, the Bing Crosby, and the Bob Hope tournaments; in football, weekly college games, the NFL championships, the Pro Bowl, the East-West Shrine game, the Rose Bowl, the Cotton Bowl, the Sugar Bowl, the Senior Bowl, the Gator Bowl, the Blue-Gray game, and Canada's Grey Cup game; in baseball, the game-of-the-week and the all-star game; and in basketball the NBA game-of-the-week and the NCAA and NIT tournaments; in tennis, the national championships and the Davis Cup matches; and in boxing, the Patterson-Jackson heavyweight title bout.

But I never did a World Series play-by-play, although I had a pre-game show. Usually I played a sort of backstage role, getting special events in connection with the series properly lined up. The busiest day was the last one, when we had to have cameras set up in the winning locker room for interviews with the heroes of the moment.

The series I remember most vividly was 1960, when the Pirates and the Yankees went seven games. I headed downstairs at the top of the seventh inning of the final game to set things up in the Yankees' locker room, since they were leading. Then Hal Smith hit a home run to put the Pirates out front, so I supervised the complicated equipment move into their locker room, right next door. Just as we completed the job, the Yankees tied the score at the top of the ninth, but we decided to stay in the Pirates' room. It was a lucky guess, for Bill Mazeroski hit a homer in Pittsburgh's half of the ninth, and the Pirates were in.

Not long after that the Yankees fired Casey Stengel as manager, replacing him with Ralph Houk. Stengel was then seventy years old. Along with millions of other baseball fans, I was sorry to see him go.

I was sorry too that I had never had a chance to know him better. I had met him many times, but never traveled with him or spent much time with him. I would have liked to be closer to him, as I had been to so many other great sports figures over the years. It was, I decided, too late now. Casey was retiring from baseball. He would always be just a name to me, a hero from a distance.

I didn't know the half of it.

Chapter 5

"Talk
to
You
Later"

I WAS pleased when I heard in the spring of 1961 that Mrs. Charles Shipman Payson, the former Joan Whitney, and M. Donald Grant had become the heads of a syndicate to form a new National League club for New York, but I really didn't think it would have anything directly to do with me. My interest was as a fan. New York had been a one-team town since the Giants and Dodgers left in 1957. It was high time the city got back into the National League.

In May, after a contest to select a name for the new team, Mrs. Payson called newsmen together at her home, held up a slip of paper, and said, "I like this one. The Mets."

"Okay," someone said. "Let's go, Mets."

My first contact with the new team came six months later, during Macy's annual Thanksgiving Day parade of floats. The

Mets had a float, on which there were a floral diamond and a big baseball with Casey Stengel's name in large letters in the center. In front of the ball were Casey himself and other members of the Met party. Along with Ed Herlihy and Buster Crabbe, I was in the NBC crew that broadcast the parade. We went over our plans during the week, and by Thanksgiving we were all set to go.

Even though I had had no connection with the Mets, I got involved in a typical Met incident. Ed Herlihy, who knew me well, was supposed to introduce me to the television audience when the Met float came into view. He introduced me all right, but the words didn't come out the way either of us expected.

"And now," he said, "to describe the baseball float for you, here is NBC's ace sports announcer, Leslie Nelson."

That stopped me, and I'm sure it stopped him, too. He had never called me Leslie before and never did again. The very thought of the Mets must have confused him.

A couple of weeks later, during the annual winter baseball meetings in Miami Beach, someone yelled across the hotel lobby, "Hey, Leslie!"

It was Joe Garagiola, now one of the Yankee announcers, with whom I had worked on the game-of-the-week. He was one of the many people I knew who had watched the Thanksgiving float broadcast. He still calls me Leslie.

The first person ever to connect me with the Mets was Charlie Bianco, a newsdealer at Grand Central Station from whom I always bought papers on my way home. At that time our family lived in Crestwood, in Westchester County. Charlie, who had read about me somewhere, was one of the few nonprofessionals around town who knew I did baseball's game-of-the-week for NBC. Most New Yorkers thought I was primarily a football announcer, since the game-of-the-week was never seen or heard within range of major-league cities. Charlie stopped me one night and said, "I'm going to nominate you to broadcast the New York Met games."

I thanked him and didn't give it another thought. I was happy in the job I had. Besides, the Met job was one of the most sought-after in the history of baseball broadcasting. I learned later that they had over a thousand applications and something like 250 audition tapes. Not only professional announcers, but former ballplayers, managers, and coaches, as well as a guy who billed himself "the voice of the Black Hills of South Dakota," offered their services.

Practically everyone in the Met organization, from Mrs. Payson and Donald Grant down, spent all spare time listening to tapes. George Weiss listened, and Johnny Murphy, his assistant, and Tom Meany, the publicity director, and Lou Niss, the traveling secretary, and the people at Rheingold, especially Al Moore, the vice president in charge of public relations, a former major-league ballplayer himself. But I guess the one who listened most was Norm Varney of the J. Walter Thompson agency, which handled the account for Liebmann Breweries, makers of Rheingold Beer.

Because the sponsors had to approve the final choice of the Mets, Varney quarterbacked the search for a three-man team of two career announcers and a baseball man. During the autumn of 1961 he must have heard auditions in his sleep.

He still hadn't made up his mind by Christmas. About then I began to get phone calls from him at NBC. I called him back a few times, but we missed connections. In the meantime I was looking forward to a tight schedule of late-season football broadcasts. I had the Giants-Packers NFL championship game in Green Bay one day, and the Sugar Bowl game in New Orleans the next. Two nights later I had a speech in New Orleans, then the Senior Bowl game in Mobile, and the next day the U.S. Bowl, an all-star game, in Washington, D.C. After a couple of commitments in New York and Philadelphia, I was going to Chicago for the annual meeting of the NCAA and Football Coaches Association, and from there to the Pro Bowl in Los Angeles. The Mets were the farthest thing from my mind.

Just before I left for Green Bay to begin my post-Christmas football safari, Varney and I finally got together on the phone.

"Can I see you today?" he asked.

"I'll be recording all day," I said.

"How about lunch?"

"I won't have time for lunch."

"Where will you be recording?" he asked.

I gave him the studio number at NBC, and we made a date to meet there when I had finished. At the end of the session he was waiting for me in back of the studio, and I led him to my office.

When we sat down he said, "What I've been calling you for is to find out if you're interested in broadcasting the games for the New York Mets."

I hadn't been interested when Charlie Bianco, the newsdealer who couldn't possibly get me the job, mentioned it to me. Now that I was talking to the man who probably could, I still wasn't interested, and I said so.

"Don't turn me down today," Varney said. "Maybe tomorrow, but not today. We have lots of announcers in mind, but not a number-one man. That's the job I want to talk to you about."

After talking some more, I agreed to phone Norm before leaving for Green Bay the next morning.

At the dinner table that night I said, "Gee, a funny thing happened at the studio today. A fellow talked to me about broadcasting the New York Met games and wanted to know if I was interested."

"Well, you are, aren't you?" Mickie said.

"Not really."

"Did you ask any details?"

"No."

My wife, who has always been much more practical than I am, looked at me and asked, "Do you think it's smart to turn down proposals you don't know anything about?"

"I suppose it isn't," I said.

"What are you going to tell this man?"

"Why, just that I'm not interested."

"Well," she said, "I think you ought to find out more about it before you walk away from it."

"Honey," I said, "if that's what you want, I'll do it."

So the next morning I called Varney and told him I *was* interested. He said he'd get in touch with me later. The next morning he phoned me in Green Bay.

"Can you get back here and meet with George Weiss?" he asked.

"Not a chance," I said. "As soon as the game here ends I'll be on my way to New Orleans."

"Talk to you later," he said.

It was a scramble getting out of Green Bay. I had to charter a plane to Chicago in time to make a series of changes that would get me to New Orleans by midnight. On the way I thought of all the places I had been, and all the planes I had chartered to get out of them in time to get to other places, and all the crazy schedules I had had—and met. And more than once on that trip I wondered why I was beating my brains out this way. At one point I leaned my head back, closed my eyes, and thought: "There must be a better way to make even this good a living." Maybe the Mets *were* the answer. If Norm Varney had been sitting beside me that night, he wouldn't have found me so hard to get along with.

But after a couple of days in New Orleans, where I waited to make that speech two days after the Sugar Bowl game, life seemed a lot easier. I was well rested and at peace with the world when the phone rang. It was Norm.

"Do you have a tape or a kinescope of any of the baseball games you've done?" he asked.

"I don't believe any was ever made," I said.

"The problem is, nobody in New York has ever heard you do baseball."

"I know."

There was a pause. Then Norm said, "Talk to you later."

After he hung up, I thought: "Well, that's that." I was relieved. I had done what Mickie asked, and now it was all over. I could stay at NBC and be happy ever after. There were worse fates.

In Mobile I had another call from Varney. "When are you going to be in New York?" he asked.

"Monday," I said. "Just for the day."

"Can you come down and talk to Weiss then?"

"Sure."

"Call me."

"Okay."

"Talk to you later," he said.

I saw George Weiss in the Mets offices on Fifth Avenue, Monday afternoon. He got right to the point. "I understand you might be available as a baseball broadcaster," he said.

"I don't know whether I am or not," I said. "We've just been talking about it."

We talked about it some more. Finally Weiss said, "What about terms and so forth?"

"I haven't had time to give it any thought."

"Why don't you think about it and give me a ring?" he said.

"All right," I said. Then, only because I had been listening to Norm Varney so often, I more or less automatically added, "Talk to you later."

"Make it tonight," Weiss said. He gave me his home number in Greenwich, Connecticut.

But I couldn't make it that night. I had to go to Philadelphia to do some taping, and I got off to a late start. All I had time for was to ask my wife to phone Weiss and tell him I'd call him from Chicago, my next stop after Philly. I was headed there for the football meetings, prior to going to Los Angeles for the Pro Bowl game. Mickie flew to Los Angeles the same day. While waiting for me to get out there, she stayed with Jerry Doggett and his wife, old friends from our Liberty Broadcasting days. Jerry does the Dodgers broadcasts with Vin Scully.

In Chicago I was tied up most of the next day in the football meetings. When I returned to my room there was a message to call Dick Young of the New York *Daily News*. That could mean only one thing. Young, one of the best-informed baseball writers in the country, must have got wind of the Met broadcasting negotiations. I learned later that his real interest wasn't me, but Leo Durocher. Because Durocher and I had worked together for three years at NBC, Young thought Durocher was also involved.

I couldn't reach him, which was just as well, because I didn't have anything to tell him. I called George Weiss, and we talked at length about details that hadn't previously been discussed. Then I phoned Norm Varney, and we talked some more but still didn't come to a firm agreement. The last thing he said was, "Talk to you later."

Before going to bed I phoned Mickie at the Doggetts' in Los Angeles to bring her up to date. When she put Jerry on, he said, "Welcome to the National League."

"I'm not in it yet," I said.

"But you have to go into it," he said. "It's New York and the big leagues. You wouldn't be thinking of turning it down."

"That's about all I've been doing for the last ten days," I said.

"Lindsey, for heaven's sake, you can't be serious," Jerry said. "There are only twenty jobs like that in the whole country. Even a new team in New York has got to be one of the best. Every guy in the business would give his right arm for it."

That gave me something to chew over. Jerry made me realize I had been playing the answer to a sportscaster's dream cooler than an offer from a little 250-watt radio station. If it hadn't been for Mickie, I wouldn't even have made a pitch for it. I remember thinking, before dropping off to sleep, that I must have been out of my mind.

Norm Varney phoned the next day with a definite offer. I asked him for another twenty-four hours so I could talk things over at dinner that night with Tom Gallery, who was on his way to Chicago from New York. After ten wonderful years with him, I wasn't about to walk out without explaining why. Gallery knew the Met deal had been cooking, and I wanted his okay before accepting it. Varney said he'd call me in Los Angeles the next morning.

Before Gallery arrived I had one more talk with George Weiss.

"Do you know a fellow from Baltimore named Bob Murphy?" he asked.

"I know a fellow from Baltimore, Boston, Oklahoma City, and Tulsa named Bob Murphy," I said, "and he's one of the best sportscasters in the business."

"Could you work with him?"

"I sure could," I said.

"Good," Weiss said. "I think we're going to hire him."

"Wonderful," I said. "We couldn't get a better man."

Not until after I hung up did I realize I had said "we."

I outlined the entire deal to Gallery during dinner that evening. When I had finished he thought a few minutes, then said, "Lindsey, I don't see how you can turn it down."

"I don't think I'm going to," I said.

I flew to Los Angeles and closed the deal orally the next morning when Varney phoned me at the Sheraton-West. His call came while I was having breakfast, and I took it on a house phone in the lobby. There were no complications. We had already agreed to terms. When he told me the Mets would like to unveil Bob Murphy and me as two of their three announcers during a press conference at Leone's restaurant the following Wednesday, I promised to be back in New York by then. For once, Norm didn't say anything about talking to me later. Come to think of it, I don't think he ever said it to me again. Maybe it's because from then on we were always talking to each other anyhow.

Two interesting things happened to me at the press conference. The New York baseball writers, who had run into me all over the country on game-of-the-week broadcasts, congratulated me as a veteran baseball announcer who had finally found a home. But the sports columnists, who seldom traveled on baseball assignments during the regular season and seldom saw me at a ball game, couldn't understand how I got the job. They heard me in New York on football, basketball, golf, and anything else that came up, but never on baseball.

The game-of-the-week broadcasts had lasted five years. The only explanation I could give was that I had had five years of out-of-town tryouts on NBC before coming into New York as a Met announcer. The columnists agreed that that should certainly be enough, since the normal tryout period for most Broadway productions was about two months.

When Tom Meany told the writers Murph and I had been selected from over a thousand applicants, I was asked when I had applied.

"I didn't," I said. "It never occurred to me."

Somebody turned to Murph and asked, "How about you? Didn't you apply either?"

"Did I apply?" he said. "I not only applied. I campaigned vigorously."

A week or so later we were joined by Ralph Kiner, who had the very best of baseball and broadcasting qualifications. During his years with the Pirates he had won or shared the National League home-run title seven straight times. After several seasons as general manager of the San Diego Padres in the Pacific Coast League, he had gone into broadcasting, doing Chicago White Sox games with Bob Elson. His fine voice and his gentle sense of humor gave the Mets broadcasting crew a touch of class.

Murph and I were delighted. As Curt Gowdy says, it's a long season and a small booth. It was a pleasure to know we would be sharing ours with a good guy whom we both admired and liked.

Chapter 6

"Ya Gotta Start with a Catcher"

T HE New York Mets were born of an administrative procedure called the "expansion draft." For a price, each team in the National League made a number of players on its major-league roster available to the Mets and the other new club in the league, the Houston Colt 45s. It was the same manner in which the American League had stocked its two new teams, the Washington Senators and the Los Angeles Angels, the year before.

By the flip of a coin with the Houston people, the Mets won first choice. They took Hobie Landrith, a catcher, from the San Francisco Giants.

Later, when I asked Casey Stengel why the Mets started with a catcher, he replied with typical Stengel logic.

"When ya build a ball club," he said, "ya gotta start with a catcher, 'cause if you don't you'll have all passed balls."

64

He used the same kind of logic when he greeted his first
Mets squad at Huggins-Stengel Field in St. Petersburg in the
spring of 1962. He gathered the boys together at home plate
and, talking as he went along, strolled down to first base. Then,
with the pack ahead, behind, and around him, he turned
toward second, still talking. After that, he moved to third, and
finally up the line back to home plate. Throughout, Casey
never stopped talking or walking. When he reached the plate,
he looked around and said, "Them are the bases. We just went
around them."

Somebody snickered, and Casey glared.

"Well," he snarled, "show me a better way to score runs."

One day someone asked Casey, "How do you figure you'll
do, managing this new team?"

"I don't know how I'll do," he retorted. "It ain't ever been
managed yet."

There's no doubt that Casey made a vast contribution to the
Mets' fantastic popularity, but there were other reasons they
caught the imagination of the New York fans so quickly. This
was a New York team, born in New York, owned by New
Yorkers, run by New Yorkers, and managed by a man who had
managed a New York team—the Yankees—to ten pennants in
twelve years. It was in a league lost to New York for four years,
and it would bring back to New York the Giants and the
Dodgers, former New York teams that still had thousands of
followers in New York.

Toward the end of spring training we prepared a television
show on film to introduce the new team to its new fans back
in New York. We called the show "Meet the Mets," and I was
to open it by asking Stengel to name his probable starting
lineup, beginning with the pitcher and ending with the outfield.
By then the lineup was pretty well set this way: Roger Craig,
pitcher; Hobie Landrith, catcher; Gil Hodges, first base; Charlie
Neal, second base; Felix Mantilla, shortstop; Don Zimmer,

third base; Frank Thomas, left field; Richie Ashburn, center field; and Gus Bell, right field. All were big-league veterans, and two, Hodges and Ashburn, had once been outstanding stars.

We were allowing a minute and a half for Casey's introduction, although I wasn't very hopeful he'd get through it in that time. It all depended on whether or not he could remember the names. His memory of faces and situations was marvelous, but names had always baffled him. This, I learned after being around him for a while, was where a lot of the Stengelese came in.

When Casey couldn't think of a name he wanted, he used any device to stall until it came to him. He'd drift off into whatever came into his head—his days at Kankakee, Illinois, where he first broke into baseball in 1910, some long-forgotten statistic, a rambling account of a game played before most of his hearers were born. The writers who knew Casey learned to spot the odds and ends for what Casey meant them to be, filler material told in his own inimitable way. Strange writers found themselves madly scribbling away while Casey just kept on going faster than they could write. None of it meant anything. He was simply trying to recall a name or a fact which temporarily eluded him.

I opened the filming of "Meet the Mets" by asking Stengel to run through his lineup. Casey got along so well in giving the answer that he had used up only about three minutes by the time he reached the outfield.

Then he said, "In left field we got Frank Thomas, who hit twenty-five home runs last year in Chicago, two in Milwaukee gets him twenty-seven, hit balls over buildings, he's got experience and power, very good, we can use him. In center field we got Richie Ashburn, who's one of the quiz kids in Philadelphia, gets on base two hundred times a year, which is excellent, delighted to have him on our side, and in right field we got five or six fellas is doing very excellent. . . ."

I knew we were in trouble. Casey couldn't think of Gus Bell's name. Other people might stammer and stutter around, but not Casey. He paused for just a second or two, then, with the cameras grinding away, he went right on talking as he groped.

"We got five or six fellas that's doing very good, and the best played for Hornsby in Cincinnati, bats left-handed and hit .300, done very good, delighted to have him, is married, has seven kids in the station wagon he drives down here from Cincinnati where he lives . . ."

On and on rambled Casey, and there wasn't a thing the camera crew or I could do except let him talk. The minutes ticked away, but that didn't bother Casey. He was getting warm, and the warmer he got the more he talked. Even though he couldn't think of Bell's name, he got everything else right about him. Bell *had* played for Rogers Hornsby when Hornsby managed the Reds, and he *was* a left-handed batter who had hit .300 a few times, and he *did* drive a station wagon from his home in Cincinnati and he *had* seven children.

Closer and closer came Casey. "Yes, sir," he said, "he comes down here for spring training with his whole family and if he can hit for us like he hit for Hornsby, he'd ring the bell—and *that's his name, Gus Bell!*"

Casey nodded and grinned and mugged and waved, and off he went. His answer to my original question had taken twelve minutes.

When spring training ended, the Mets flew from St. Petersburg to Norfolk, Virginia, in a chartered plane. They were scheduled to play in nearby Portsmouth the following day. The plane landed on schedule, but the bus that was supposed to meet the team hadn't arrived. There was a mix-up in the arrangements. Gil Hodges and a few others took a cab down-town, but the rest of us hung around until the bus finally got there, twenty minutes late.

It started raining late in the afternoon, and while we were in the area it never stopped. The next morning when we went over to the Portsmouth ball park it looked as if the James River had been rechanneled. In some places the water was a foot deep, and it would get deeper, because the rain kept pouring down. The game was called off.

We all went back to the hotel and spent the afternoon just hanging around. Another chartered plane was taking us to New York, but it had been assigned to pick us up after the game. The poor Mets couldn't even get off the ground in Norfolk.

We sort of sneaked into New York. When we arrived at La Guardia at nine that night, nobody knew we were there. There were no bands, no crowds, no banners. Even the airline employees were unimpressed. La Guardia was being rebuilt, and we landed at a makeshift terminal which had been a hangar and office building. We got off the plane and walked single file through a maze of ropes and planks until we reached the street. Nobody cheered, nobody waved, nobody yelled, "Let's go, Mets," nobody cared, nobody knew we were there except the bus driver. This one was waiting to take us to Manhattan.

For the real veterans on the team the ride into town was old hat, but many of the younger men had never seen New York before because the teams for which they had played never came in. They peered out the window with the hungry curiosity of immigrants. When the lights of the city across the East River came into view, I heard more than one awed "oh" and "ah." Manhattan at night is a thrilling sight for anyone, and especially a newcomer. At that hour traffic was light and the bus moved fast. That night we were staying at the Savoy-Hilton, a pretty plush joint for a club that had "tenth place" written all over it. The poor Mets—not much ability, but lots of class.

We went out to the Polo Grounds the next day, because Stengel wanted his boys to have a workout there before going to St. Louis to open the season. The Mets had spent over $200,000 fixing up the ancient ball park the Giants had abandoned five years earlier. Like Norfolk, New York had had plenty of rain, and the newly resodded grass was so heavy with muck that my shoes disappeared when I stepped on it.

The workout consisted of getting in and out of uniform, running around a little, and having a look at the place. Even nature was fighting the Mets. When it was time to leave for La Guardia and the trip to St. Louis, they still hadn't played any baseball since breaking camp in Florida.

It was a quiet plane ride west. In some ways, it reminded me of the trips I had taken with combat troops when none of us knew where we were going. The ballplayers knew their immediate destination, and a look at the schedule would have told them where the team would be all season, but individually they had no idea where they were headed. Just before leaving the Polo Grounds one of them, Joe Christopher, had been ordered to Syracuse because the team had to get down to its squad limit for opening day. Others would be following him, but nobody knew who or when. Oddly enough, Christopher eventually survived all but two of those original Mets. He lasted until December of 1965, when he was traded to the Red Sox.

The stewardesses had their hands full trying to serve everyone dinner on the trip to St. Louis, so Frank Thomas volunteered to help. He went up and down the aisle, poking people in the ribs and asking "Gonnaeat?"—slurring it into all one word. He worked as hard as the girls, setting up the trays and delivering them to the ballplayers and supernumeraries. He continued to do it on plane trips all season.

I meandered up and down the aisle myself, just to talk to people. When I reached Red Ruffing, our pitching coach, who had enjoyed a great career with the Yankees, it occurred to me that he had seen more big-league baseball openers than anyone on the plane except Casey and one or two others.

"How many did you pitch?" I asked him.

"Most of them," he said.

"What about Lefty Gomez? Didn't he pitch any?"

"A few," Ruffing said. "But Lefty got so keyed-up when a new season began that he often was sick to his stomach. After the season started he was great, but he never liked opening days."

I went back to my seat wishing Ruffing were twenty years younger. We sure could have used him on the Mets.

The weather was bad in St. Louis too. It was drizzling when we landed, and the forecast for opening day, April 10, wasn't good. Met weather, it looked like. And at the hotel where we checked in we had another typical Met incident.

The boys didn't have to register, since that had already been done for them by Lou Niss, the traveling secretary. All they had to do was get their keys. There was a rush for the desk, then another rush for the elevators. Everyone tried to get into the same one. When it was packed solid, the door closed and the elevator started up. It went about two feet, shuddered, and stuck. On their first night on the road the Mets were stuck in an elevator two feet off the ground. That was the highest they got all season.

The Cardinals play mostly night games, including their season's opener, so we had all of the next day to kill. It rained intermittently, just as it had everywhere in the East, but there was hope for a ball game, and we headed for the park. Ralph, Bob, and I went up to the radio and television booths to look things over. As the rain didn't stop, the ball game never got started. An hour later we were back at the hotel with another twenty-four hours to kill.

"We must be good," someone said. "Nobody wants to play us."

The Cardinals were happy indeed to play them. The weather cleared the next day, and the Mets finally got off to the first season of their existence. The very first inning was a harbinger of things to come. The Mets failed to score in their half. The Cardinals got a man to third in theirs—and Roger Craig, the Met starting pitcher, balked him home. That's how the first run in Met history was scored against them. The Cardinals won, 11–4.

We went right from Busch Stadium to the airport for the flight back to New York. We faced a short night because there would be a ticker-tape parade for the Mets down Broadway at noon the next day. The last previous ticker-tape parade had been for John Glenn, the astronaut. When Stengel heard that, he remarked, "We ain't never gonna get that high. I'll settle for ninth place right now."

Wake-up calls came at nine-thirty a.m., and the ballplayers had to meet in the lobby of the Manhattan Hotel in uniform. I was having a quick breakfast in the coffee shop when Jim Marshall joined me. People stared at him, but nobody asked him for his autograph. Half of them probably didn't yet know who the Mets were. The other half must have thought he was an actor or something. What would a real big-league ballplayer be doing in uniform in the coffee shop of a downtown hotel at ten in the morning?

The parade turned out to be a fantastic success. The ballplayers rode in threes and fours in open convertibles with identifying placards taped to the sides. Julie Adler, then the Met promotion director, had stocked each car with plastic baseballs to be thrown to the crowd along the way. Casey Stengel, bowing and waving, was in the lead car with George Weiss. Casey, the flying baseballs, and the Met uniforms left no doubt in anyone's minds just what kind of parade this was. The crowd got into the spirit of the thing, and pretty soon baseballs flew in one direction and ticker tape in the other.

The welcome was all out of proportion to the importance of the recipients. Seats once occupied by the Lindberghs and MacArthurs and Eisenhowers were now filled by a collection of young men almost completely unknown to the people welcoming them, but that didn't matter. This was a real New York welcome to New York's newest big-league team, the first indication that the fans weren't going to be just impersonal spectators but a part of the ball club.

If the Mets should ever win a pennant at some distant future date, they won't get a wilder welcome than this vagabond collection of cast-off athletes got that April day in 1962. The air was white with tape and plastic baseballs as the city honored a ball club which had played only one game and lost that. At City Hall everyone got out of the cars and went to sit on a platform behind a podium where Mayor Robert F. Wagner made the welcome official. He gave a speech, Casey gave a speech, everybody laughed and whistled and yelled and applauded, and a good time was had by all.

When it was over, the ballplayers went to the Polo Grounds for a workout, while Ralph, Murph, and I were taken to the Waldorf Astoria by Phil Liebmann, president of the Liebmann Breweries, to watch the judging for Miss Rheingold. I arrived home that night feeling pretty good. I asked Mickie how many people she knew had ever taken part in a Broadway ticker-tape parade at noon and a beauty contest in the afternoon. She agreed, not many.

I still had something of a swelled head when I arrived at the Polo Grounds at ten o'clock the next morning. Even at that hour there was quite a bit of traffic on Eighth Avenue. The first National League ball game to be played at the historic old horseshoe park at the foot of Coogan's Bluff since 1957 was obviously going to draw a pretty good crowd.

I headed for the press parking lot behind the north side of the stands, but traffic was so heavy I couldn't get through. The police were routing all traffic into the big public lot, and that included me. I didn't have anything to identify myself as being with the Mets except a sticker on my car. When a cop refused to let me through to the press lot, I said, "I'm the Met broadcaster."

"I don't care who you are," he said. "You go where everybody else goes."

So the great big important guy who had spent the previous noon being honored in a ticker-tape parade and the previous afternoon as a guest at a beauty contest drove into the public parking lot and paid his dollar just like everyone else. The mighty sure fell far fast.

I almost had to pay my way into the ball park too. At the press gate, the attendant took a lot of convincing before he would let me in. I had to show everything from my auto license to my old NBC identification card before he would accept my story. That collapsed my ego completely.

The opening-day ceremonies started an hour before the ball game. I stood at the public-address microphone at home plate, fighting the echoes, which were particularly bad at the Polo Grounds. It took so long for what you said to be transmitted to the speakers that the sound came back at you while you were saying something else. If you started listening, you forgot how far you had gone and what you had said. The Polo Grounds acoustics have thrown some of the world's most stirring orators.

I introduced Mrs. John McGraw, widow of the immortal Giants manager of another era, and Mrs. Charles Shipman Payson, the Mets' principal owner. Mayor Wagner gave a speech of welcome, as did Donald Grant, the Mets' chairman of the board. He asked everyone to buy Rheingold beer, an understandable request, since Rheingold's radio and television money was all the Mets had seen up to that moment.

The Met starting pitcher was Sherman (Roadblock) Jones.

Roadblock had been a doubtful starter for a very odd reason. On the bus going from the hotel to the airport in Norfolk he had hurt an eye while lighting a cigarette, and there was a question whether he might be able to start by opening day.

He started, but he didn't finish. The Pirates won, 4–3, with Roadblock in the showers at the end. He didn't make it to the end of the season, now that I think of it. I wonder whatever happened to him.

It had been a cold and frustrating, yet historic, day. New York was back in the National League. The Mets were a reality, though losing. I stopped in at the clubhouse, where I found everything normal. Casey was holding court for the writers. I listened a few minutes, then walked back to the public parking lot where I had left my car. Somebody had broken into it and scattered papers and maps from the glove compartment around the front seat.

At least they hadn't taken the car. I drove home feeling more like a winner than a loser.

Chapter 7

"We Love You, Mets"

THE phenomenon of the Mets, their popularity, their huge attendance, their wild-eyed fans, the appeal they have to New Yorkers—and to people elsewhere in the country as well—has been one of the most overexplained sports miracles of recent years. Sociologists, psychologists, and psychiatrists, as well as ordinary mortals, talk glibly of the Met syndrome and what it means.

Of course it isn't all that complicated, although there are several reasons for the Mets' being what they are. There's no question that they filled a gap left by the departure of the Dodgers and the Giants in 1957—especially the Dodgers. Today the Dodgers are one of baseball's most successful organizations, a strong, colorful, perennially victorious team in a huge metropolis. They are to the National League what the Yankees were to the American.

But there was a time when the Dodgers were everybody's doormat. They were losers and clowns. Crazy things happened to them, like leaving three men on third on a double and having outfielders like Babe Herman get hit in the head by fly balls. People who went out to watch the Dodgers, cheering their few successes, laughing at their mistakes, expected to see them lose.

The same people continued to watch them when they started winning. The fans didn't have as much to laugh at, but they had more to cheer about. And they could pick games apart, make yesterday's heroes into today's goats, tell the world how a losing game should have been won, brag about a winning game. Jackie, Duke, Gil, Campy, Preacher, Peewee, Cookie, the Carls, Oiskine and Furillo, weren't simply idols. They were Brooklyn incarnate.

Fans went to the ball park with pennants and noisemakers and said and did as they pleased. They were uninhibited, untrammeled by convention. Win, lose, or draw, Dodger fans were Dodger fans, different from anyone else in New York, different from fans anywhere in the country. They went to the ball park to have a good time.

Although not quite so demonstrative, Giant fans were just as devoted to their ball club. They loved their heroes and were proud of a heritage dating back to the days of John McGraw. They loved their horseshoe-shaped Polo Grounds, with its short foul lines that invited Chinese home runs traveling only 279 feet to left field and 257 to right. They worshiped at the shrine of Carl Hubbell and Mel Ott and Leo Durocher and Alvin Dark.

They differed from Dodger fans in one very significant respect. Dodger fans went to Ebbets Field whether the team won or lost. Giant fans went to the Polo Grounds only when the Giants were winning. By 1957 the Giants were losers. They had to move to survive.

The loss of both teams at once to the West Coast took

National League baseball out of New York altogether, leaving thousands of fans without a ball club. A few drifted over to the Yankees, but only a few. It was fact, not fancy, that Dodger-lovers and Giant-lovers were, for the most part, Yankee-haters who wouldn't be caught dead in Yankee Stadium.

The trouble with the Yankees was that, although you could see magnificent baseball played by a magnificent team, you had to do it with decorum. You could cheer, even boo, but you couldn't bring pennants around, or noisemakers, or anything else that might draw attention away from the field and into the stands. The Yankees were remote, a proud, haughty team sufficient unto itself. The fans who watched them were expected to be spectators, not participants.

Yankee Stadium was a place where you took your guests, your clients, your out-of-town visitors. It was part of the New York scene, like the Empire State Building and Grant's Tomb. Any baseball fan in for a brief visit didn't consider his trip complete without seeing the Yankees in their own back yard. It was time well spent, but you had to behave while you were there. You didn't go to the stadium to make a riotous racket or have a load of laughs. You went in the same spirit that you went to the United Nations or the Statue of Liberty. You were going to see something, not to take part in it.

It's altogether different with the Mets. Their fans have no awe, no reverence, no deep stirrings of the soul. At Met games, the fans are part of the spectacle. They go out as much to watch other people as to watch the ball game. They laugh and wave flags and signs and sing songs and write poetry and enjoy themselves, much as they did at Ebbets Field when the Dodgers were there. And the Mets inherited much of the stadium personnel that had once run Ebbets Field, such men as Jim Thomson, business manager, and Matt Burns, who runs the physical property at Shea Stadium.

The Mets had something to offer the serious fan, too—the

chance to see National League baseball, a chance that had been denied him for four years. I've always contended that New York is fundamentally a National League town anyhow. The National League got there first and had two teams there for more than half a century. All those thousands of fans, starving for idols, suddenly had some place to go again. Dodger and Giant buffs couldn't wait for their old favorites to visit New York. To this day games between the Mets and either the Dodgers or the Giants are sellouts or near sellouts. In 1965, the Dodgers and Giants attracted 674,188 to Shea Stadium, an average of 42,137 per game. At first the fans didn't know just where their loyalties lay, but now there's no doubt. They want the Mets to win even against yesterday's heroes.

Whatever the Mets do, their fans never go home disappointed or unhappy. I once asked my old friend Charlie Bianco, the newsdealer who first suggested that I become the Met announcer, "Are you a Met fan?"

"Sure," he said.

"Do you go out to watch them play?"

"As often as I can."

"Why?" I asked.

"Because I have fun," he said.

Everyone who goes to see the Mets has fun, and no one has more fun than their principal owner, Mrs. Charles Shipman Payson, unless it's the people associated with her. They sit down near the Met dugout on the first-base line, yelling and waving and clapping and laughing along with everybody else.

Mrs. Payson, sister of John Hay (Jock) Whitney, former ambassador to the Court of St. James's, is listed as a vice president of the Mets. The chairman of the board, Don Grant, represents her, as he has in various enterprises for years. When Mrs. Payson, a lifelong baseball fan, had a minority holding in the old New York Giants, Grant represented her on the board of directors. At the board's meeting to consider the move from New York to San Francisco in 1957, there was one dissenting vote. It was Don Grant's.

The executive vice president of the Mets is G. Herbert Walker, Jr., son of the donor of golf's famous Walker Cup. Frederick K. Trask, Jr., a business partner of Mrs. Payson's, is a director of the club, and Luke B. Lockwood, also associated with Mrs. Payson's interests, is the secretary-treasurer. The club is actually run by George Weiss, its president.

They are the Mets' most rabid fans. Nothing but urgent outside matters keeps any of them away from the ball park when the Mets are at home. And I'm told that when the club is on the road none of the officers is far from a radio. When not at home or in cars, they wander around with transistor sets going full blast.

Joan Payson and her brother, as owners of the Greentree Stables, have been prominent in racing circles for many years. One day when the Mets were playing elsewhere, she went to Aqueduct, armed, as usual, with her transistor radio. When her horse won the feature race, she appeared in the winner's circle to congratulate the trainer.

Just as she started to shake hands with him she heard my voice rise, meaning that something good for the Mets was happening in the ball game. "Congratulations," she said, putting the radio up to her ear.

"Thanks," the trainer retorted. "And what's the score?"

The Mets began the 1963 season with eight straight losses. They finally won their first game of the season in the Polo Grounds on a hit by Ron Hunt. This made him the first Met hero of the year (they have no villains, only heroes). Mrs. Payson got so excited that she sent Hunt a huge bouquet of roses the next day.

The only trouble was, Hunt was allergic to roses. He came out to the field with a runny nose and red eyes, but he played. His first time up he hit a double, sliding into second base.

By then his eyes were streaming. Time had to be called while
Hunt sopped up his rose allergy with umpire Augie Donatelli's
handkerchief.

Music, lyrics, and parodies have been a part of the Mets
almost from the beginning. One spring evening in St. Petersburg, the second year of the team's existence, the Mets and the
Cardinals, who also train there, were given a joint party by
the city. The formal part of it was over early, but somebody
had an accordion and somebody else began to sing, and pretty
soon Mrs. Payson and a whole group of us were off in one
corner in a songfest.

Cookie Lavagetto and Solly Hemus were Met coaches then,
and Choo Choo Coleman was catching—or at least trying to.
Somebody produced a parody on Allan Sherman's wonderful
parodies. We sang them so often that night, I remember these
lines to the tune of "Frère Jacques":

> Lavagetto, Lavagetto,
> How's by you, how's by you?
> How are things at first base?
> Get us out of last place.
> You're nice, too, you're nice, too.

> Solly Hemus, Solly Hemus,
> How's by you, how's by you?
> How are things at third base?
> Haven't seen a Met face.
> You're nice, too, you're nice, too.

> Choo Choo Coleman, Choo Choo Coleman,
> How's by you, how's by you?
> Memory never lingers,
> He has to count his fingers.
> You're nice, too, you're nice, too.

When the party broke up in the wee hours of the morning, Don Grant said, "If we can have this much fun now, think of how it will be when we're *winning*."

You can't be associated with the Mets without something of them rubbing off on you. Consider the case of Russ Byrd, a St. Petersburg entertainer who often appeared at the Colonial Inn on the beach, where the Mets made their spring headquarters. He worked hard on a parody of "Hey, Look Me Over" to present at a Met party at the Colonial one night. When the time came to sing it, this experienced entertainer, who had been around the business for years without freezing, forgot the lyrics. A Met at heart, if I ever saw one.

Later, Russ gave me those lyrics. Here's how they went:

> Hey, look us over,
> We are the Mets.
> We're George's darlings,
> Casey's little pets.
> Don't pass the plate, boys,
> Don't pass the cup.
> Remember whenever you're down and out
> The only way is up.
> And we'll be up like the Dodgers,
> The Giants we'll beat.
> Just give us time
> To get up on our feet.
> We're a little bit short
> Of the elbow room
> But let us get us some,
> Then, look out, world,
> Here we come.

Okay, so it's doggerel. But you should see some of the stuff that comes in from fans almost every day. Typical was the rock-and-roll lilt of these lines:

We love you, Mets, oh yes we do, oh yes we do,
   oh yes we do, oh yes we do-oo-oo—
We want you to win more games for us too-oo-oo—
We give you cheer like this too-oo-oo—
Our Mets are the bets.

Met fans, clad in T shirts and slacks, dungarees and sneakers, business suits, silk dresses, cashmere sweaters, and mink stoles, are relaxed when they come to the ball park. When their Mets pull a bloop they laugh and clap their hands, like parents watching a little child trying to walk. He takes a step and falls down, and they laugh and applaud him for trying; then he takes another and falls down and they laugh and applaud some more. When a Met fan laughs he's not making fun of his boys—he's laughing because they are funny trying. The laugh is one of fondness, not ridicule.

Everybody fell in love with the Mets at first sight. They were hopelessly outclassed, but they were funny and you had fun watching them. That first year, 1962, the betting was even that they'd be out of the pennant race by Mother's Day, which is about a month after the season starts. They nearly were, too.

The first Mother's Day the Mets were in town, Red Smith, the great New York *Herald Tribune* sports columnist, said to Kay, his wife, "This is your day. Anything you want, you can have. And anything you want to do, we'll do."

"Thanks, honey," Kay said. "I'd like to go to the Polo Grounds and watch the Mets play a doubleheader."

And that, at her own request, was where the wife of one of the nation's top-ranking sports columnists spent Mother's Day that year.

There are lots of fringe benefits to being associated with the Mets in a capacity such as mine. One night around six o'clock I was pinched for speeding on the Cross-Bronx Expressway, en route to the Polo Grounds. After I had pulled over to the shoulder of the road, one of the officers got out of the patrol car and walked back to mine. I gave him my license and registration, and he went back to talk to his partner. After a while he beckoned to me.

When I reached him, he asked, "What's your job?"

"I'm a broadcaster for the New York Mets," I said.

"I thought so." Then, returning my papers, he shrugged and said, "Hell, buddy, you got enough troubles."

Late one summer afternoon Mickie met me downtown for dinner and a show. We decided we'd like to see the musical *Oliver*, but my ticket broker couldn't get a thing. There was a theater party that night and everything was sold, even the house seats. We strolled around a bit, then, finding ourselves in the vicinity of the theater, decided to try the box office.

The line was short because the fellow in the cage was just shaking his head and saying no to everyone who approached him. He had his head down when I reached him, asking, "Anything for tonight?"

"No, no," he said. "Nothing at all."

I started to leave, but just then he looked up, peered at me, and said, "Hey, wait a minute." As I turned back, he exclaimed, "I'm a *Met* fan!"

"Fine," I said. "What about tickets?"

"Got you two right here," he said. "Center section, fourth row. You stop by about eight o'clock when you come in tonight and check with me again. I might be able to improve on them."

"How can you improve on center section, fourth row?"

He just kept on staring at me. Finally he shook his head and murmured, "I'm a Met fan and you're the Met announcer. How about that?"

About a year later, during the World Series, I stopped at the Metropolitan Opera House to see if I could pick up a couple of tickets for *Rigoletto*. When I reached the head of the line the man at the box office said, "The only thing we have in the orchestra is in Row Y. They aren't the best, but they're unobstructed."

"If that's all you have," I said, "I'll take them."

I paid for the tickets and turned to go, but another man in the cage stopped me.

"Just a second," he said. "I'm a *Met* fan." He had that same look on his face as the fellow at *Oliver* had. "Why aren't you out at the ball park?" he asked.

"The Mets didn't make the World Series," I said.

"That's right. Let me see those tickets you just got."

I passed them to him and he disappeared. A couple of minutes later he returned and said, "Give me two more dollars and here are your tickets."

They were seventh row center, about as good as you can get. I thanked the man and went off, thinking how you find Met fans in some of the most unlikely places.

Francis Robinson, the publicity director of the Metropolitan Opera, was a close friend of Tom Meany. Whenever Meany wanted someone to sing at special Met occasions at the Polo Grounds or Shea Stadium, he phoned Robinson. Some of the world's most priceless voices have sung the national anthem, then yelled encouragement at the Mets.

Expensive talent comes free when the Mets are involved. At Dodger Stadium in Los Angeles one time, Joe Gallagher spotted the late Nat King Cole and asked him to come up to our booth. Cole had once done Rheingold commercials, but those days were well behind him. Nobody would have blamed him for refusing Joe's request, but he didn't. Before the game was over, he was singing the commercials live between innings and having a wonderful time.

In 1962 it rained the first time the Dodgers ever came to New York to play the Mets. There's no problem on radio when rain interrupts a ball game. All you have to do is let the studio play recorded music until it stops. But on television it isn't that easy.

You can't just play music. And if you switch to other programing you'll never get your audience back. So, as a matter of policy,
when you're on TV during a baseball rain interlude you just
stay on and do what you can to entertain the fans. The longer
it rains the tougher it is, and I was having a tough time filling in.
There was a slight commotion behind me, and someone slid
into the next seat, whispering, "I heard you were in trouble, so
I thought I'd come up."

It was Danny Kaye. At that time all three networks were
romancing him, but he was still reluctant to go on television.
He put on his first one-hour spectacular that rainy night in our
booth at the Polo Grounds—for Met fans.

You see Met fans everywhere. I went out to the Twentieth
Century-Fox studios in Hollywood for lunch with publicist
Chuck Panama one day, and later to a set where a movie was
being made. To my surprise, the stage hands crowded around
me and kept coming back to talk whenever they had a free
minute or two. They were Met fans.

During the baseball season it's impossible for me to walk
along any main street in Manhattan without having two or
three cab drivers, usually with fares, pull over and yell, "Hey,
Linds, what're we gonna do about our Mets?" It happens
with policemen, firemen, doormen, shoeshine boys, subway
attendants . . .

Subway attendants. One day I was in the news department
of NBC, talking to Leonard Probst, the drama critic, when I
said, "Well, I have to get the subway out to the ball park."

"The subway?" he said. "Television announcers don't take the
subway. Television announcers take taxis and helicopters and
rented cars."

"Not Met television announcers," I said. "We take the
subway."

"But don't you get recognized?"

"Sure I get recognized. They're all Met fans."

Two minutes after I step into a subway train there's a baseball discussion going on. It's still going when we reach the ball park, and I suppose it would be going all night if I didn't have to go up and get to work.

In 1963 the Mets went to West Point to play an exhibition game with the cadets, as the Giants used to when they were in New York. As we marched into the mess hall for lunch, the corps began humming, then their voices swelled into a rousing rendition of "My beer is Rheingold, the dry beer."

Casey Stengel read the orders of the day and knocked them dead. The boys who weren't Met fans when we arrived had crossed over by the time we left, and since then Met scores have been reported to the cadet corps at evening chow.

One night in 1962, right after Duke Snider lined a home run into the right-field seats to beat the Cardinals in a wild finish at the Polo Grounds, I went out to meet some people from NBC on the Eighth Avenue side of the ball park. They were yelling and whooping it up along with everyone else. When they saw me coming, they howled a happy greeting. And right there, in the middle of the milling crowd of Met fans on Eighth Avenue, they gave me a cigarette lighter engraved: "To Lindsey Nelson, because NBC loves your Mets."

Who doesn't?

Chapter 8

The Worst Chef on Television

MY friends were surprised when I resigned from NBC to take the Met job. They asked me repeatedly why I had sacrificed a national audience for a local one, why I had swapped coast-to-coast exposure for New York exposure.

I suppose the answer is much the same as an actor's when he drops everything for a part in a Broadway show. Baseball broadcasting is entertainment, and New York is the entertainment capital of the world. There are ten million people within daily hearing range and many more millions of visitors. Besides, while once-or-twice-a-week baseball is fine for a reporter, everyday baseball is a way of life that I intensely enjoy.

Don't misunderstand me. I'm not underestimating the importance of national audiences. They meant a great deal to me before I joined the Mets, and they do today. I still work for NBC and other networks in the baseball off-season, telecasting football and other sports, and I hope to continue to indefinitely.

But no network could give me what the Mets do. A baseball broadcaster has the best showcase in the city. During the season he's on the air almost every day, at prime time in the evening, on Sunday afternoons, anywhere from two hours to five at a stretch. His identification with the ball club is absolute. He is as well known to the fans as the team's brightest star, and, since he doesn't have to depend on his pitching arm, his batting eye, or his legs, the chances are he'll last much longer. All this is of great value to a sports announcer in any big-league city. In New York, it's priceless.

I was not the first announcer faced with this decision. Red Barber resigned as CBS sports director to stay on the baseball beat. Vin Scully gave up numerous network assignments for Dodger baseball. Some announcers can't understand this situation. One day I ran into Ted Husing, who asked me about Mel Allen. When I said he was doing very well, Husing shook his head and said, "I never thought baseball would be that important."

Different announcers have different techniques, and crews in different cities handle their games differently. In a one-team town, for example, an announcer can be a cheerleader, referring to his team as "we" and exhorting it on to victory the way a fan would. He knows his listeners feel just as he does.

Bob Murphy, Ralph Kiner, and I can't do that. New York is the only city in the country that ever had three major-league baseball teams in town at once. Each had its own separate, avid, dedicated following. And today each of the two teams in town has its own separate, avid, dedicated following. If we showed partiality to the Mets on the air we'd lose every transient fan who ever tuned us in. The millions of people who come to New York every year have their own favorites. They tune us in to see how their ball clubs from home are doing. The Chicago visitor, for example, might fall in love with the Mets, but he's still a Cub or a White Sox fan. The Cincinnati visitor might have a great time at Shea Stadium, but he's primarily interested in the Reds. Whatever our personal feelings, we must broadcast Met games without prejudice.

Not that we aren't prejudiced. You can't live and work and spend months on end with the same group of men, have friendly family contacts with them, eat and talk and travel and constantly associate with them, and build up mutual friendships with them, without hoping they'll win. All three of us are Met fans. We dream of that happy day when the Mets will be pennant contenders. We must be objective. You might say we're objectively very much in favor of the Mets.

When Ralph and Murph and I met in St. Petersburg as a broadcasting unit for the first time in 1962, we spent many hours discussing among ourselves and with Norm Varney and Joe Gallagher just how we would handle the broadcasts. We knew the Mets would be hopelessly outclassed by everyone except Houston. There wasn't anything we could do from the radio or television booths to make them look any better. The scores would tell the story. There would be no sense trying to fool the public into thinking this was really a better ball club than it looked. It was sure to be bad, and to stay bad for a long time.

So we decided to play it straight. We agreed simply to report events as they happened in the manner of their happening. As it turned out, this in itself often was hilarious. All Murph or I had to say was, "Throneberry drops it," and Met fans back home fell out of their seats laughing. All Ralph, speaking from the depths of his experience as a former ballplayer, had to say was, "He threw to second instead of first," and Met fans broke up. We didn't have to paint the lily.

Varney and Gallagher figured out our assignments and rotation that first spring in Florida, and we've never changed them. On the opening night of the season I worked the first four innings on television and Murph worked the first two on radio. Ralph did the third and fourth innings on radio and the fifth and sixth on television. Murph did the fifth and sixth on radio, and the seventh, eight, and ninth on television, while I did the last three on radio. Because Ralph had pre-game and post-game television shows when the Mets played at home, his assignments there stayed constant, but Murph and I switched the second night, and we alternated each home game throughout the season. On the road, where we didn't always televise, Ralph was included more in the rotation.

We didn't think anybody would be particularly interested in this schedule except us, but we were wrong. We're always getting letters and phone calls from fans complaining that they hear the same announcer all the time, or somebody works more than somebody else, or there's too much repetition. I once had a letter saying, "Mr. Nelson, please don't finish the broadcasts. You're a jinx. Every time you finish a broadcast the Mets lose. Let somebody else finish."

I didn't know what to tell the man. He was quite right. I *did* finish every game, on either radio or television. And the Mets *did* lose most of their games.

Repetition in baseball broadcasts is constant and necessary because most listeners cut in and out, especially in New York, where so much baseball is on both TV and radio. The Mets televise more games than any team in the history of the major leagues. A fan might listen to a car or a transistor radio for a few innings, then go home and see the rest of the game on television. Or he may have time to tune in only occasionally. Or he may switch to something else and then switch back. Comparatively few people begin at the beginning of a ball game and catch it on the same medium all the way through to the end. It's a constantly shifting audience, with somebody always missing something he wants to be filled in on. That's why there's so much repetition.

Some fans never listen to baseball on radio and some never watch it on television, but the announcers work both media. The ball club and the sponsors want this because it strengthens the identification, and the stronger the identification the more effective the salesman. The sports announcer has two primary functions: to describe the event and to sell products. He's like any other entertainer in radio and television. Perry Como sings songs and sells products. Johnny Carson tells stories and sells products. Hugh Downs reports the news and sells products. This is the nature of the business.

Commercials are delivered at regularly scheduled times. Baseball is the most perfect sport for radio and television because there's a natural break at the end of each half-inning. Sometimes this break is filled by a commercial, sometimes by comment about the game or about personalities in it, or by scores of other games, or by something in connection with the home team, the visiting team, or any other team. Whatever he does in those breaks, the announcer is selling either the product of his sponsor or the game of baseball.

When there is more than one sponsor, the commercials may be constant or rotated. If they are constant, commercials of the same sponsors are given in the same spots each night; if rotated, the sponsor who starts tonight's game might finish tomorrow's. This is all worked out in advance by agreement among the sponsors' representatives.

It's not unusual in the broadcasting business for a sponsor to buy an entire package and then sell off some of it to another sponsor, which is what happened with the Mets. Liebmann Breweries got the original rights on behalf of Rheingold Beer, then sold a portion to the Brown and Williamson Tobacco Company, makers of Viceroy and Kool cigarettes. It was agreed to alternate sponsorship, with Rheingold beginning on opening

day, since it was the principal sponsor. As it happened, opening day in 1962 was rained out. The producer had planned to
open with Viceroy the next day in accordance with the original
agreement, but this didn't sit well with Phil Liebmann, who
had the very reasonable objection that his product should lead
off the telecasts, since he was footing the bulk of the bill. Brown
and Williamson saw the point, and the switch was made just
before we went on the air. It meant that Norm Varney had to
rewrite the cues and lead-ins at the last minute in longhand
while talking back to New York on the phone, but everything
worked out. After the first hectic night we've had no occasion
to change that many cues after arriving at the ball park.

That first spring in St. Petersburg, Murph and I filmed some
commercials outdoors for later use. We had a very windy week,
resulting in some interesting complications. In one pitch, Bob
sat at a table with a bottle of beer on it. As he talked of the
virtues of Rheingold he was supposed to pick up the bottle
and hold it up in front of him. Just as he reached for it, a gust
of wind blew it along the table. He stretched out farther, and
the bottle again went out of his reach. He just managed to
grab it before it slid off the table altogether, but by that time
he was sprawled at about a forty-five-degree angle. He looked
like a guy trying to pick up a windblown hat that wouldn't
stay still.

I had a commercial in which I was supposed to pour a glass
of beer while talking. The director told me it would be most
effective if I kept making the pitch right into the lens of the
camera, rather than looking at the glass while I poured. The
wind came up just as I began, and the next thing I knew I was
swimming in Rheingold. If you think it's easy not to change
expression while beer trickles down your chest and your legs
inside your clothes, try it sometime.

I did another commercial that week, in which I wore a chef's
hat and cooked hamburgers on a grill while talking about how

well beer goes with hamburgers. The wind blew so much smoke into my face that my eyes were streaming while I tried to flip the hamburgers. We finally got a couple of usable takes out of it. Before we broke camp I had a letter from a friend, saying, "I thought you'd like to know that you're famous as the worst chef in television."

Any number of people have expressed their sympathies to me for being one of the broadcasters for a losing team. It really isn't that bad. We may have a losing team, but we have the best audience. Besides, the Mets, who don't win much at home, win even less on the road. This cuts down our work load in the broadcasting booth. When traveling, we seldom have to do the last half of the ninth inning. The home team usually wins in eight and a half.

We get quite a bit of mail—and criticism—about calling pitches. How, people ask, can we tell a slider from a curve? How do we know if a batter hits a home run off a screwball, a change, a knuckler, or a fast ball? Newspapermen frequently contend that it's impossible to call pitches correctly from a booth. The answer is that when we don't know what a pitch is we don't try to call it. But we do know what certain pitchers can do, what pitches they have at their command, what pitches they are most likely to throw in given situations. And we can tell something from the way the catcher handles a pitch, or the way the batter reacts. We can't call all the pitches all the time, but we can call some of them some of the time.

Some people, especially old-timers, object to the way we broadcast no-hitters. With the Mets, we're likely to see more no-hitters than most broadcasters because the Mets go into more batting slumps than anyone else. Jim Bunning even had a perfect game against them in 1964; not a single man reached first base.

There's an old superstition in baseball that if you mention that a pitcher has a no-hitter going he'll lose it. This started in the dugouts years ago, and at one time it was so strong that the mention of a no-hitter was practically a federal offense around a ball park. The ban spread from the dugouts to the press boxes to the stands, and eventually into the radio booths. Younger writers and some ballplayers no longer worry about this vestige of a bygone age, but thousands of older baseball followers still think it's heresy to mention a no-hitter while it's being pitched.

Of course the man in the broadcasting booth has no control over whether or not a pitcher will pull off a no-hitter. We agreed very early that we would report one just as we would report anything else that happens in a ball game. You can't be restricted by an old wives' tale when you're talking to millions of listeners who are tuning in and out and should be kept informed of what has happened. Furthermore, by not telling the fans a pitcher has a no-hitter going, you're doing a disservice to your sponsor by not building your audience.

In 1962 Sandy Koufax of the Dodgers pitched a no-hitter against the Mets in Los Angeles. We mentioned several times that he had one going. He came on the air with us the next day, and I asked him about the superstition of not mentioning a no-hitter while it was in progress.

"We talked about it all through the game," he replied.

Then he told me that in the eighth inning, while they were working on a Met batter, his catcher, John Roseboro, came out to the mound and said, "Don't walk this guy, but don't lose your no-hitter either."

We had quite a lot of mail, including a letter from a man from Brooklyn who wrote: "Why did you call that no-hit game the way you did? You were very unsportsmanlike. You should know that you don't mention a no-hitter after the sixth inning."

In June of 1965 Frank Lary of the Mets and Jim Maloney of the Reds got into a great pitching duel in Cincinnati. In the fifth, I mentioned on the air that Maloney had a no-hitter going; then, when Ralph relieved me, I joined Joel Nixon, our executive producer, in an adjacent booth. Pat Harmon of the Cincinnati *Post* dropped by in the seventh and asked, "Have you fellows mentioned that Maloney is pitching a no-hitter?"

"Certainly," I said. "We're still mentioning it on just about every pitch."

"Some broadcasters don't touch it because they're afraid of jinxing the pitcher."

"Well," I said, "I know announcers who say they don't mention no-hitters out of deference to an old dugout superstition. We take the position that we're not in the dugout. If anything we said in the broadcasting booth could directly affect anything happening on the playing field, we'd be worth a lot more money that we're getting."

I didn't realize then that Waite Hoyt, the Reds announcer and an old-time Yankee pitching star, never mentioned no-hitters on the air. I knew Harmon was building a story on broadcasting no-hitters because he took notes as I talked. I told him about Sandy Koufax in 1962, and about our mentioning Bunning's perfect game in 1964, and I said that an announcer owes it to his fans to tell them about no-hitters in the making.

By this time it was the ninth inning, and there was still no score for either team and there were no hits for the Mets. Murph had relieved Ralph, who was sitting beside him in our radio booth. I invited Harmon to come into the booth and listen to Murph. The first thing we heard him say was, "Maloney is working on a no-hitter."

The ninth ended with the game still tied, and Ralph moved back in to do the play-by-play. The Mets went through another hitless inning, giving Maloney a ten-inning no-hitter, but the Reds couldn't score off relief pitcher Larry Bearnarth in their half of the tenth, so it was still 0–0. At that point it was my turn to take over the broadcast back to New York.

I was hardly settled in the chair behind the microphone when

Johnny Lewis of the Mets smashed a leadoff home run, the first hit off Maloney. Bearnarth held the Reds scoreless in their half of the eleventh to give the Mets an astonishing 1–0 victory.

The next day the headline over Pat Harmon's story read: HOYT CONCEALS NO-HITTER. N.Y. ANNOUNCERS DIDN'T.

He quoted Hoyt: "The fans—if they're real fans—know what's happening. In my day as a player, they never talked about a no-hitter on the bench while it was going on. It wasn't mentioned in the press box. I didn't want to stir up anything."

All through the game Hoyt had talked around the phrase "no-hitter." He had called Maloney out of this world, a great pitcher, a real pitcher. He had said Maloney's pitching was impeccable. He told his hearers that the score was 0–0 and they should sit tight, implying that something special was occurring. And at the end of each inning he had given the Reds' runs, hits, and errors, but not the Mets', because then he would have had to say they had no hits.

While I admired Harmon's industry in digging out a good feature story, I was somewhat upset. The last thing I wanted to do was get into a hassle with Waite Hoyt, whom I considered a good friend and the nicest of people.

I felt much better after the second edition of Harmon's paper came out. This carried an additional story, headed: HOYT ABANDONS OLD CUSTOM, and quoted Hoyt as follows:

"In view of last night's game we've decided to abandon the old custom of not mentioning a hitless performance while it is in progress. We've given it a good deal of consideration and have finally decided that we've been catering too much to the old-time fans, who we felt knew immediately what the situation was during the broadcast by the way we handled it. But we realize that many people joining the audience at different times during the game were entitled to know the facts."

I have mentioned that one of the advantages of being a

baseball announcer is lengthy exposure during prime time. Consider what happened to us on Sunday, May 31, 1964.

The Giants, in town for a doubleheader that started at 1:05 p.m., won the first game, 5–3. They were leading in the second game until Joe Christopher of the Mets hit a home run over the left-field fence in the last of the seventh to tie the score at 6–6. The score was still tied at the top of the eighth. At that point Ralph Kiner left the booth to prepare for his postgame show in the television studio downstairs. I was on radio and Murph on television with the game still deadlocked at the end of the ninth.

I figured it would end in an inning or two, so I stayed on radio, leaving Murph on television. Radio is a far tougher job, because you must describe everything in detail. On TV, much can be left out because the audience can see what's going on. I didn't mind talking for a while longer; after all, that's my business.

But neither team scored in the tenth, or the eleventh, or the twelfth, or the thirteenth, or the fourteenth, or the fifteenth. By then, having been going steadily all day, I was getting hoarse. Ralph, down in the studio, knew both Murph and I could use help, but he didn't dare leave because the game might end any minute. After the fifteenth, Murph and I swapped places.

On and on went the ball game, through the sixteenth, the seventeenth, the eighteenth, the nineteenth, the twentieth, and still neither team could break the deadlock. Around that time we got an unexpected bonus of new listeners when John Daly, after being introduced on the popular weekly television show "What's My Line?" said, "I've just been watching the most incredible ball game. The Mets and the Giants are in the twentieth inning." Nobody knows how many people then switched from his show to ours, but it must have been thousands.

As the game went beyond the twentieth with still no decision, we began hoping it would get up past the major-league record of twenty-six, a 1920 marathon between the Brooklyn Dodgers and the Boston Braves that ended in a 1–1 tie. Also, we were approaching midnight. We wanted to be able to say the Mets started a doubleheader in May and ended it in June.

But in the twenty-third inning, just after eleven o'clock— "What's My Line?" ended then, and Daly could get back to his television set—the Giants broke the ice and scored two runs. The Mets, held scoreless in their half of the inning, finally lost, 8–6.

It was eleven-twenty p.m. when the game ended. The teams hadn't matched the twenty-six-inning record, but they had broken just about every other record for uninterrupted big-league baseball. Their thirty-two innings in the two games were the most ever played in one day. The seven hours, twenty-three minutes consumed in the second game made it the longest in time, and the nine hours, fifty-two minutes altogether made this the longest doubleheader.

And our more than ten and a half hours of continuous broadcasting, including the post-game show that Ralph Kiner finally got around to doing, was the longest dual radio-television announcing job in baseball history. We had done thirty-two innings on radio and thirty-two on television, for a total of sixty-four innings of baseball.

That was my longest day of live baseball, but I'd had plenty of stretches just as long during my Liberty Broadcasting System days. And in September of 1964 I had a fourteen-hour work day that reached practically across the country. I spent the afternoon televising the Pitt–UCLA football game in Pittsburgh for NBC, then flew to Los Angeles in time to pick up the Dodgers–Mets game at Dodger Stadium at eight p.m. the same day.

Once you reach a certain plateau in this business, you are

offered more work than you can handle. But it takes so many years to get there that it's hard to turn down high-paying jobs that suddenly drop into your lap. Some top-flight announcers can't resist the temptation. For a long time I couldn't either. In self-defense I had to learn to say no. This is a tough word for anyone to use at the prices available, but the alternative is practically to kill yourself with work.

Because sponsors now demand names that don't have to be explained to the public, it's very hard for an unknown announcer to break into the big time. The easiest way is to jump right from the field to the microphone. More and more, the trend is to hire well-known athletes with good voices. The best jobs are offered to the limited number of professional announcers with the biggest reputations. Yet there are plenty of men around the country who could do as well if they had the chance. How do they get the chance? I often wonder, for the circle is vicious and the circumstances are frustrating. If the sponsors won't take you because they don't know you, then you can't work. And if you can't work, how are the sponsors going to get to know you?

I ran into that problem in my early years at NBC. As assistant sports director, my job was largely administrative at first, and I did very little work on the air. Time salesmen used to drop into my office and say, "We'd love to have you do some of these big games, but we can't get sponsors to accept you because they don't know you."

I finally did the NCAA college football play-by-play in 1955, but only after the salesmen had been pitching me for three years. The following summer, Mike Dann, then in charge of sports sales, said one day, "I think you're finally over the hump."

"What makes you think so?" I asked.

"Well," he said, "the last few years I'd go in to sponsors to sell games and they'd say, 'Who's going to do them?' and I'd say, 'Lindsey Nelson,' and they'd say, 'Who's he?' Then I'd have to go into a big long spiel explaining who you were and how much experience you had had, and it still took a long time to sell you.

"This year," he went on, "I make a pitch and say Lindsey Nelson is going to do the games, and they say, 'Who's he?' and I say, 'He's the fellow who did the games last year,' and they say, 'Fine.' That's why I think you're over the hump."

So I suppose that's the answer. Unless you're an athlete with a big name, the best way to get this year's jobs is to be the guy who did last year's.

Chapter 9

Homer

S OMETIMES I grieve for Homer, now fat and dog-
forty as he lives in comfortable retirement on Long
Island. For a while he was to the Mets what Charley O. later
became to the Kansas City Athletics, a living, throbbing animal
mascot. I would say, however, that Homer was quite clearly
superior to Charley O., even though Charley O. had a bigger
reputation.

To begin with, Homer was more truly a Met than Charley O.
was an Athletic. Charley O., the property of owner Charles O.
Finley of the Athletics, was simply a mule with a baseball cap
on his head. Homer was a beagle that could run bases.

Homer also had more class than Charley O. The mule
watched games from an enclosed area beyond center field in
Kansas City's ball park, where Finley's sheep used to graze.

Homer had a platform behind the screen at the Polo Grounds. It was set on top of four box seats, which were bought and paid for. Charley O. lived in a stable. Homer lived in the Waldorf Towers. Charley O. had an ordinary, garden-variety horse handler. Homer had a trainer imported from California.

Homer was the brainchild of Phil Liebmann, who decided that a beagle of quality and intelligence could bring welcome publicity to both the Mets and Rheingold Beer. Liebmann's original idea was to call the dog "Mr. Met," but that name had already been pre-empted by the ball club, which gave it to a cartoon character that symbolizes the Mets. The name "Homer" was appropriate enough. If the Mets didn't get any home runs in a game, they could always say they had at least one in the ball park.

When I first saw Homer, he was slim and sleek and smart. His trainer was a quietly efficient man with the rather improbable name of Rudd Weatherwax, who had trained Lassie for the movies and television and who was brought in from Hollywood to make a Met fan, and later a baserunner, of Homer. He did a magnificent job.

As Homer watched the Mets from the eminence of his position behind home plate, he did everything but stand up and cheer. Whenever we put the camera on him, as we did from time to time during the games, he held up a banner in his mouth. It read, "Let's go, Mets," and it started the craze for banners among Met fans. After a while, people brought banners like, "Bethpage Loves the Mets," "Scarsdale Loves the Mets," "Everybody Loves the Mets," and they have been bringing banners to Met games ever since.

Homer might have taken a bow for it all if he had realized how much he had to do with this fad, which goes on and on and I hope will last as long as the Mets do. In the very early days of the Mets, fans at home, seeing Homer on television, obviously decided that if a dog with a suite at the Waldorf, a Hollywood trainer, and four box seats for every game could carry a banner, so could they.

Pretty soon Homer got as much fan mail as anybody on the Mets, and it all came to us. Every time Homer appeared on camera, Murph or Ralph or I referred to him as the Mets mascot. We answered all the letters, because we didn't want anyone slighted, signing Homer's name. We thanked people for writing and told them how much we (Homer) appreciated their taking the trouble.

While Homer usually sat on his platform, we once had him come up into the booth at the Polo Grounds to make an appearance with Bob Murphy. We picked Murph because dogs —especially beagles—fall in love with him on sight. He's a bit on the round side and very likable. Homer sat quietly on his lap while Murph delivered a commercial. Ralph helped all he could. When the commercial ended he said, "The one on the left is Homer."

Homer had a beautiful face, for he was a finely bred beagle with all kinds of impressive ancestors in his pedigree. He and Rudd Weatherwax got along like ham and eggs. Weatherwax was a marvelous trainer, and Homer did practically everything with the sort of flair you might expect from a more or less permanent resident of the Waldorf. He could do all kinds of tricks, like waving the banner back and forth in his teeth, growling out a bark without dropping it, mugging for the cameras, and bowing his head so his Met cap would show more clearly. Kids went nuts about him, crowding around his box, calling him, petting him, and doing just about everything but ask him for his autograph.

We put him on television a couple of times a game. When it was time for Homer to go on, his young admirers crowded around, grinning and yelling and waving banners. It got to be one of the highlights of the ball game for the small fry—and a few of the large as well.

The big moment of Homer's life was supposed to be when he ran around the bases on Rheingold Day in 1963. This was scheduled for the Polo Grounds between games of a double-header, when Homer would share the spotlight with the candidates for Miss Rheingold. First we would introduce the girls; then Homer would put on his act.

Weatherwax really worked on this one. He didn't want anything to go wrong in front of all those people, so he began training Homer early. I never saw any of the initial training, because Weatherwax couldn't work when the ballplayers were there. He took Homer to the Polo Grounds mornings and made him go over and over his race around the bases for hours at a time.

On the day before the climactic event we had a rehearsal. I was master of ceremonies, using a microphone near home plate. When it was time for Homer to do his stuff, I announced, "And now, ladies and gentlemen, Homer, the Met mascot, will run around the bases."

I heard Weatherwax, who was holding Homer at the plate, whisper something, and off went the beagle. He ran down the line to first, then turned and headed for second. There he turned again and dashed to third, then made the last turn up the third-base line and across the plate. It was a perfect perform-ance, and everyone who saw it cheered like mad.

That was the rehearsal.

Now it was Rheingold Day, with a good crowd out at the Polo Grounds to see the girls, the ball games, and Homer circling the bases. First we introduced the girls, who smiled and waved and walked back and forth near the plate. When Rudd Weatherwax brought Homer down to the field from the box behind the plate, there were cheers from Homer's thousands of fans. After they died down, I made my announcement, just as I had the day before at the rehearsal.

Weatherwax whispered the magic words into Homer's ear and, while the cheering swelled into a roar, Homer took off. He dashed down the first-base line, went over the bag, and turned toward second. His very act of turning was enough to set off the fans to more heights of wild cheering, banner-waving, and hand-clapping.

Having seen all this the day before, I must admit I wasn't particularly impressed. I had great faith in both Homer and Rudd Weatherwax. This, I figured, would be—for Homer—a routine performance.

The dog approached second base. He touched the bag, although I couldn't tell with how many feet, and then, without slowing up, suddenly turned toward the plate. And, while Weatherwax stood transfixed and thousands of loyal Homer fans, including this one, broke up completely, Homer cut across the pitcher's box and into the waiting arms of his trainer, who by now was reconciled to the inevitable.

Homer was a pretty expensive luxury. Keeping him in the Waldorf cost something like $18,000 a year, which was more than keeping most of the ballplayers cost. The four box seats at the Polo Grounds were somewhere around $800 more for the season. On top of that were Rudd Weatherwax's fee, which was not a small item, and daily transportation between the hotel and the ball park. You couldn't expect a beagle of Homer's class to ride in the subway.

Despite the cost, I felt he was worth every penny, and I was disappointed when, after Rheingold switched agencies, it was decided to eliminate Homer from their budget. The Mets had troubles enough keeping ballplayers who couldn't run the bases properly, so Homer bowed out of the picture after two years.

But not completely.

Al Moore, vice president of Rheingold, took Homer to Mut-
tontown, Long Island, to keep as a pet. He was a poor one at
first, for after two years of rigid training he was a nervous wreck.
But after he realized that Moore didn't expect him to do anything but just be a nice beagle, that's exactly what he became,
and today he's a marvelous pet.

In 1965 we had an old-timers' day at Shea Stadium, and how
could the Mets have an old-timers' day without Homer? No
longer sleek and slim, or, I fear, even very smart, Homer was
still such a handsome animal that we decided to put him on
television. The only time Homer had ever been in a booth was
the day he sat on Murph's lap at the Polo Grounds. He had
never seen the Shea Stadium booth, where everything is plushly
comfortable and the woodwork beautifully polished.

Although he lives very well in Al Moore's lovely home, Homer
was two whole years away from his Waldorf days and not used
to such luxury any more. After we put him on the highly waxed
table where our television microphone is, I grabbed his collar
to hold him steady while I started delivering a commercial.

Reading from a cue card off-camera, I began, "Rheingold is
as good—" when I felt a quivering and a terrific tugging move-
ment. Homer, obviously unhappy on that smooth tabletop,
was trying to get off.

"—to your taste—" I went on . . . tug, tug, tug . . . *jerk*.
Now I was half out of my seat.

"—as it is to your thirst—'"

It was impossible to keep the camera on both of us. Since
Homer is prettier than I, you would think it would have stayed
with him, but he wouldn't stand still. They kept the camera
on me, but by then I was cackling so hard I could barely get
the rest of the pitch out. The bit ended in a shambles, with
Homer finally getting his way.

It was, of course, a mistake having me try to do the job in
the first place. Murph was Homer's true love, and I'm sure

Homer would have cooperated with him. Besides, after his exercise stretching for bottles in St. Petersburg, Murph is much better equipped than I to go stretching for beagles. From now on, the job is his.

Chapter 10

"Casey Stengel, Doin' Very Good"

WHEN Leo Durocher and I were teaming up on baseball broadcasts for NBC in 1959, we went to Washington one day for a game between the Senators and the Yankees. Casey Stengel was managing the Yankees then, and he was having a rare season: this was one of the few years a Yankee team of his lost the pennant. With things going badly, he was a bit irascible. When we reached the ball park in Washington, we discovered that he had ordered his locker room closed to everybody but ballplayers and Yankee personnel.

"What do we do now?" I asked Durocher.

"We gotta get the lineups," Leo said. "So we go in. Maybe Stengel will throw us right out into the street, but we can't lose by default. Come on. Let's go."

Nobody stopped us and nobody threw us out after we got in.

Durocher wandered around talking to ballplayers, and I headed for Casey. Already in uniform, he was sitting on a trunk, staring at the floor, with his arms folded and his legs dangling. He didn't seem to want to talk to anybody, so I hung back, waiting for him to notice me.

He finally looked up and said, "Like your job?"

"Yes, sir," I said. "I like it very much."

"Guess you want the lineup, huh?"

"Yes."

Saying, "Come on," he hopped off the trunk and led me to his office. There he reached into a pocket of his street suit and pulled out several sheets of hotel paper with perhaps a dozen different batting orders written in pencil. He had obviously been wrestling a long time with the problem of getting more power into his lineup.

He sat behind the desk, and I pulled out my score book.

"Leadin' off and playin' second base, Bobby Richardson," Casey said.

I wrote down Richardson, while Casey stared out the window. Then he said, "Would you believe it, a year ago Gil McDougald would be leadin' this league in base hits and leadin' this league in runs batted in, and now he can't seem to get a hit 'cause when he hits 'em they don't go out like they usta but up like they do and somebody catches 'em? But he's gonna get a hit one day and if he did he might get two or three and if he did it might be three or four and he'd ruin somebody. Rub out Richardson and put down McDougald."

So I rubbed out Richardson and put down McDougald.

"Battin' second and playin' left field, Norm Siebern," Casey said.

While I wrote down Siebern, he asked, "Siebern fall down yesterday?"

"No, sir," I said.

"Siebern didn't fall yesterday," Casey said, "he'll fall down today. Seems to me Siebern is gonna fall down on some big play almost every day now and you can't catch a ball lyin' on your back in left field it's very difficult. Rub out Siebern and put down Howard."

So I rubbed out Siebern and put down Howard, while Casey went on, "Mantle is battin' third and Skowron is fourth and in fifth I got nobody but Larsen if he'd hustle would be playin' the outfield 'steada pitchin' and be makin' $55,000 a year 'steada what he's makin' and we'd be winnin' some games."

"You want me to put down Larsen?" I said.

"No, because he won't hustle and he can't hit and he don't make $55,000 and we can't beat nobody," Casey said.

I didn't get out of there with a full lineup for half an hour, but in that half-hour I learned more about Casey than I had ever known before. The thing that stuck with me more than anything else was that he fundamentally made sense, despite the hilarious confusion of his speech. Later, when I became associated with him on the Mets, I saw this sort of thing repeated time and again.

One day in the first year of the Mets' existence Bing Miller, once a great Philadelphia Athletics outfielder, dropped by the dugout to see Casey.

"Casey," Miller said, "your team isn't winning. It isn't even looking good, but that doesn't seem to bother you too much. You look as though you're keeping your health."

"I'll tell you about that," Stengel said. "When a good team don't win, the manager oughta worry, but I ain't bothered too much about this team ain't winnin', 'cause there's somethin' wrong with it."

Casey was the funniest man any professional sport ever knew, but he was dead serious about baseball, more serious than any other baseball figure of modern times. He covered up this intense feeling with his pixie sense of humor, but that made him no less the complete baseball man. This was his business, his pleasure, his hobby, his life. He didn't play golf, he didn't go to the movies, he didn't take naps, he didn't sit alone in his hotel room. When he wasn't at the ball park he wanted to talk about the game, so he could always be found where people gathered—in lobbies, in restaurants, in bars, in press rooms. You never had to go looking for Casey. He was always right at hand.

I think it was a bit of a shock to him to learn just how utterly hopeless the Mets were that first year of their existence. He had had bad teams before—the Brooklyn Dodgers of the mid-thirties and the Boston Braves of the late thirties and early forties—but his last team before the Mets had been the Yankees, with whom he had won ten pennants and seven world's championships. He was used to the problems of trying to figure out how to win. It had been years since he had wrestled with the problems of trying to figure out how not to lose.

At first Casey wanted to be sure his players knew the proper moves, on the theory that, if they knew what to do, they would go ahead and do it. He talked endlessly of how men in various positions should react to given situations. He had a fantastic knowledge of every facet of the game, and he knew exactly how to cope with almost any given situation.

Only the Mets couldn't cope.

There was, for example, the time he told them how, with men on first and second base, they might get the man at first. "Sometimes," Stengel said, "if that runner on first thinks you're makin' a play at second he'll be a spectator and pretty soon he's so interested in what's goin' on at second you can pick him off easy."

One day in San Francisco the Giants had men on first and second, and the Mets pulled the play perfectly. The pitcher was looking at the man on second, trying to hold him close. Sure enough, the man on first got so deeply interested he forgot he was standing three feet off the bag. The pitcher whirled and threw to Ed Bouchee, the first baseman, who had the base-runner caught flatfooted.

The only trouble was, Bouchee dropped the ball.

Later in the season the Mets hit into a triple play at Chicago. When they reported at St. Petersburg the following spring, we asked Casey if there was anything special he wanted his men to learn.

"Not drop the ball," he replied. "And we got to work on our defense against triple plays."

One night in 1962 pitcher Roger Craig started getting racked up by the opposition. After somebody belted a double off him, Casey came out of the dugout, swinging his arms, spitting on his palms, slapping his hands together, and gimping along on his unsightly underpinnings. He was still about fifteen feet away when he yelled, "Well, doctor, what seems to be the trouble?"

"I'm having a little trouble holding the ball," Craig said. "My fast ball is all right, but the curve seems a little slippery. I can't grip the ball right, I don't know why."

Casey pointed to the mound and said, "You're standin' on two tons of dirt. Why don't you rub some of it on the ball?" Then he turned and went back to the dugout.

Late in the 1963 season, during a game at the Polo Grounds, Tracy Stallard twice got belted for home runs into the right-field seats. After the second one went in, Stengel stopped the game and went out to the mound.

"Doctor," he said, "at the end of the season they're gonna tear this joint down. The way you're pitchin', that right-field section will be gone already."

Opposing hitters broke all kinds of batting records before the Mets were through with the Polo Grounds. Up to the time they arrived there, the only man ever to hit a ball into the center-field bleachers had been Joe Adcock of the Braves, who did it against the Giants in 1953. Nine years later, against the Mets, Lou Brock of the Cubs and Henry Aaron of the Braves belted balls into that distant sector in one week.

In mid-season I was up on the dais at our old-timers' dinner with Casey on my left and Bill Terry, who had succeeded John McGraw as the Giants manager, on my right. Casey leaned across me and said, "Bill, what was your pitchin' strategy at the Polo Grounds?"

"You've got to pitch everybody outside," Terry replied. "With those short foul lines and that great big deep center field, you can't ever let a hitter pull the ball. Make him hit it to center."

"We been tryin' that," Casey said, "and they're hittin' 'em into the center-field bleachers."

Traveling with Casey was an education in human relations. Everybody knew him, and many claimed he knew them. Despite his sharp tongue, Casey was a true gentleman, courtly to the ladies (to whom he had enormous appeal) and courteous to the men. Often an old-timer would be sitting in the dugout hours before a game, waiting to talk to him. Whether Casey actually had ever met the man or not, he was always polite and friendly.

Although his memory for names was terrible, his recollection of faces and associations with those faces was absolutely uncanny. One day in Chicago a man who must have been over eighty approached Casey.

"You won't remember me," he said, "but I knew you years ago."

"Just talk a minute," Casey said, "and I'll tell you whether I remember you or not."

"I'm from Kankakee," the man said. "I used to be in the restaurant business."

Casey had started out in baseball at Kankakee in 1910. He peered at the old man, then said, "Don't tell me that. It wasn't the restaurant business. You had a diner. Isn't that right?"

"That's right."

"You used to sell meal tickets to the ballplayers for five dollars a week, right?"

"Right."

"And I'll tell you one more thing," Casey said. "That league folded up in the middle of the week, in July. And you still owe me two dollars and seventy-five cents on my meal ticket."

Casey could remember an inconsequential detail from fifty-two years back, but he couldn't remember a name two minutes after he heard it. Neither can many of us, but Casey couldn't even remember one when he was in close daily contact with its owner. He was always mixing up the names of people whom he saw every day. It was a constant surprise to him to learn someone he had been calling by one name actually was someone else.

Our broadcast producer, Joe Gallagher, had been the Yankees statistician at one time during the period when Casey was their manager. On the road he roomed with Jim Woods, then Mel Allen's broadcasting partner, and the two were always together. When Gallagher joined the Mets, Casey called him Woods.

One night a group of us went out to dinner in St. Pete. Later Casey began telling stories about the Yankees. After one of them he said to Gallagher, who sat across the table from him, "You remember that one, don't you, Woods?"

"Sure, Casey, I remember," Joe said. "But why do you call me Woods?"

Casey looked at Joe as if he were crazy. And for a long time after that he didn't call Joe anything.

One of the original Mets was a pitcher named Bob Miller, for whom the club paid the Cardinals $125,000 in the expansion draft. For reasons best known only to himself, Casey always referred to him as Nelson. He knew I was the announcer and Miller the pitcher, but our names just didn't mean anything to him. Maybe he linked them together because each had six letters.

One day after Casey announced that "Nelson" would start the game, a writer said, "Casey, you keep saying Nelson and I'm sure you mean Miller."

"Well," Casey retorted, "I may say Nelson, but when I say Nelson, Miller knows he's working, and my coaches know he's working, so what difference does it make?"

His habit of calling ballplayers "doctor" must have dated back to his college days. Casey spent several years in dental school in Kansas City, where he was born and brought up. He quit one day when he absent-mindedly pumped a patient in his chair all the way up to the ceiling. The man, who had acrophobia, was not only in pain but scared to death.

"Couldn't you let me down a little?" he moaned.

Casey let him down all the way and then walked out. "Even my mother thought I was a lousy dentist," he told me.

Chris Cannizzaro, a catcher who was in the first Mets expansion draft, baffled Casey. He always referred to Cannizzaro as "Canzoneri," a name he knew, since Tony Canzoneri was a former boxing champion. Whenever Casey said "Canzoneri" everyone, including Cannizzaro, knew whom he meant. As far as Casey was concerned, that was all that counted.

Coming north from St. Pete the first year, Casey was asked by a Baltimore writer for his lineup for an exhibition game against the Orioles. The newspaperman had a Met roster to check off the names.

"At first base, Hodges," Casey said. "At second, Canoe. At short—"

"Wait a minute, Casey," the writer said. "Who at second?"

"Canoe, Canoe," Casey said impatiently. "And at short—"

"I don't find any Canoe," the writer said.

"Look, I'll show you," said Casey. He took the writer's roster and pointed to the name, Rod Kanehl. To Casey, he was Canoe then and forever.

There were so many injuries in spring training in 1962 that the busiest man on the ball club was the team physician, Dr. Peter La Motte. At a dinner a few weeks after we returned home, somebody asked Casey what he thought of the expansion draft. His answer had everyone rolling in the aisles.

"We got some very excellent fellows that we selected them 'cause they were college men," he said. "We figured if we couldn't find 'em that was good we'd get 'em that was smart and we checked on the college men and we selected 'em very carefully 'cause they was from Johns Hopkins which is a very brilliant place except we found our men was from the clinic instead of the college and our most valuable man was the orthopedic surgeon which, thank heavens, we did not pick up in the expansion draft but got him on Park Avenue."

Casey's sense of public relations was superb. No writer ever walked away from him without a story. It might not be the story he went after, but it would be something usable and printable. With the Yankees and later with the Mets, Casey always talked proudly of "my writers," the men who traveled with the club and to whom he gave the real news breaks. But he talked endlessly to visiting writers and broadcasters, who flocked around him wherever he went. Casey was undoubtedly the most interviewed man in the United States. Not even the President was ever under such a continuous barrage of questions requiring off-the-cuff answers.

Actually, Casey never gave any direct answers. He didn't have to. Somewhere or other in one of his marathon monologues were the answers to just about all conceivable questions. Of course the interviewer had to dig the one he wanted from a maze of unrelated digressions in a language of Casey's own. Those who knew him well knew when to take notes and when to relax. Those who didn't went mad trying to get everything he said down on paper. This was impossible without a tape recorder or a high-speed secretary.

Casey was the most subtle practical joker I've ever seen. He had a wonderful gag which he often pulled while being interviewed in the dugout. He waited until there were so many people around him that some had to stand on the steps because there wasn't room for them anywhere else. At this point, perhaps in answer to a question, he would suddenly talk in a very loud voice, giving two or three highly quotable lines.

Then he would begin to talk a little softer, continuing to decrease the volume of his voice until it was down to a whisper. By then the men on the steps would be leaning so far forward they were practically falling on their faces. While they frantically asked, "What did he say?" Casey, his bright blue eyes gleaming but his face otherwise expressionless, would casually get up and walk away.

He liked to enumerate his points while looking for the one that counted. "Now so-and-so is a very excellent player, and that's one and you got to go to two." Then he'd make another statement, finishing, "Now you gotta go to three." Sometimes he'd get all the way up to fifteen or twenty before he reached what he really wanted to say.

It all boiled down to the fact that it didn't matter what you asked because you'd always get the same running, complete, all-inclusive answer. One day an announcer from Cincinnati came over to Casey in Florida for an interview. Casey waited until the tape was rolling, then, before the announcer could say a word, took the microphone and began, "Casey Stengel, St. Petersburg, Florida, doin' very good as manager of the New York Mets and we got this lineup." He went right through his batting order, commenting on the men as he went along and answering about every possible question an interviewer might ask. Finally he said, "Casey Stengel signing off from St. Petersburg, Florida," and handed the microphone back. The announcer had a perfect interview without a word of his own.

Casey's doubletalk provided him with a great defense against ticklish questions. Other public figures, in sports, entertainment, politics, or whatever, would respond with a "No comment," but not Casey. He realized there were three basic objections to "No comment": it doesn't take up any space in the papers, it is utterly colorless, and it infuriates newspapermen. Instead of "No comment," Casey always replied with generous portions of his own brand of "filler" material. He never answered the question, but he sent everyone away with something. That was how he avoided the stigma that "No comment" would have brought.

One of Casey's greatest assets is his wife, Edna, a delightful lady and a perfect foil for him. When the two are together, they interrupt each other constantly, for Edna, who tells stories at great length and in detail, likes to talk as much as Casey. They would have provided the script-writer of a family situation comedy with endless material.

One spring Casey took Edna along when the Mets played a three-game exhibition series in Mexico City. As they were leaving to come home, there was a mixup at the airport because Edna had misplaced her identification papers. She had to be escorted back and forth from one office to another, so she told Casey to keep an eye on the luggage.

Everybody was standing around Casey, who sat on a big suitcase. Edna must have come by a dozen times, while Casey made remarks like, "No trouble gettin' her into the country, but we're havin' a terrible time gettin' her out," or, "They don't like me none, but they sure like Edna."

On one of her trips across the lobby, Casey said, "Edna, I been watchin' these three bags all the while."

"There were four," she said, and then she was gone.

Since Edna came from an extremely well-to-do family, she never had any financial worries. One night in West Palm Beach, Florida, with his wife on the dais, Casey was talking to an audience made up mostly of ballplayers, about the virtues of the baseball pension fund.

"Y'see," he said, "in early years when we was playin' we didn't have this pension plan so we didn't know that when we quit playin' we was going to get paid in retirement years like you fellows, and if you was married like I was and you had a wife with relations, you'd know what the situation was going to be."

At this point Edna stood up and said, "Mr. Stengel, don't worry about your wife's relatives." Then she sat down while Casey calmly finished his speech.

Chapter 11

Every
Man
a
Hero

HUEY LONG rode to glory in Louisiana on the slogan, "Every man a king." From the day they met at spring training in 1962, the Mets rode to glory on the unspoken slogan, "Every man a hero."

It took very little to make a Met a hero. Met fans in the making were so hungry for ballplayers to lionize that spring-training games produced favorites even before the club reached New York. The first of these was a twenty-five-year-old catcher named Clarence Coleman, whose nickname was Choo Choo. So sparing of words he made Gary Cooper sound like a chatter-box, Choo Choo, who called everyone "Bub," had a vocabulary consisting largely of "Yup," "Nope," and "Hi."

He won an everlasting niche in Met history in the second game they ever played, an exhibition against the Cardinals at

Al Lang Field in St. Petersburg. The Cardinals had shut them
out in the first game the day before. They were on their way
to doing it again until Coleman came up as a pinch-hitter in
the eighth inning and belted a two-run homer off Johnny Kucks.
When the Mets went on to win a 4–3 victory, Coleman was
home free.

He was a tough interview, but the writers could cover that
up in their stories. We couldn't, yet we had to get him on the
air sooner or later because everybody was talking about him.
Before putting him on a pre-game television show, Ralph Kiner
asked Murph and me how we thought he should be handled.
After discussing the problem, we decided the best thing to do
would be to start off by asking him how he got his nickname.

"There's bound to be a story behind it," Ralph said. "If
Choo Choo will tell it, I'll be all set."

There was no problem getting Choo Choo on the show. He
readily agreed to appear with Ralph before the game, and when
the cameras were turned on him he grinned like a movie star.
After the commercial, Ralph confidently introduced him, then
asked, "Choo Choo, tell us first where you got that nickname."

Choo Choo, looking right into the camera and still grinning
happily, replied, "I dunno."

Choo Choo roomed with Charley Neal, one of the few real
big-league ballplayers the Mets had. On the day Neal reported
for spring training the next year, he walked to the batting cage
to join a group of us standing there, pointed to Coleman, and
said, "I'm going over and say hello to Choo Choo. I roomed
with him last year, and I'll bet he won't even know my name."

We thought he was kidding, so we followed him over. Neal
stuck out his hand and said, "Choo Choo, it's good to see you."

"Hi, Bub," Choo Choo said.

"You know my name, Choo Choo?"

"Yup."

"I'll bet you don't," Neal said.

"I know ya all right," Choo Choo said. "You're number four."

When the Rheingold advertising account was transferred back to Foote, Cone and Belding in 1964, the agency man working with us at St. Petersburg was Clarence Thoman. One day the phone rang in the locker room at Huggins-Stengel Field. It was the agency in New York. When Herb Norman, the equipment man, answered, he thought the caller asked for Clarence Coleman, not Thoman. He went to the door and called, "Choo Choo, here's a call for you."

Choo Choo picked up the phone and said, "Hello, Bub."

"Clarence?" the caller asked.

"Yup."

"We want to check these contracts with you. We've got to get them in the mail Tuesday. That third paragraph—is that exactly how you want it?"

"Yup."

"You've had a chance to read it thoroughly?"

"Yup."

"And you want it just this way?"

"Yup."

"If we get them in the mail today, do you think you can have them signed and back here in plenty of time?"

"Yup."

By this time the man in New York knew something was wrong. "Are you sure this is Clarence Thoman?" he asked.

"Yup," Choo Choo said.

Then, handing the phone back to Herb Norman, Choo Choo made one of his longer speeches.

"Man is crazy," he said.

At the opposite end of the spectrum from Coleman was Ken MacKenzie, a Canadian-born left-handed pitcher with a Bachelor of Science degree from Yale. One day, after bringing him in from the bullpen in relief, Casey Stengel handed him the ball and said, "Pretend they're the Harvards."

When the first season ended, MacKenzie got into a salary hassle with the Met brass. As he walked out of a session with George Weiss, he remarked, "It's kind of discouraging to realize I'm the lowest-paid member of the Yale Class of 'fifty-six."

Which prompted someone in the office to add, "With the highest earned-run average."

One of the problems facing Lou Niss, the traveling secretary, was the fact that the Mets had two pitchers named Bob Miller, one right-handed, the other a southpaw. Niss solved it by rooming them together.

"That way," he said, "anybody phoning Bob Miller won't disturb anybody else if he gets the wrong one."

Later, in a discussion about the Mets' many problems somebody said, "The only department in which the Mets lead the National League is in Bob Millers."

The most legitimate hero the Mets had was Gil Hodges. A great ballplayer with the Dodgers, he was a big favorite around town because he moved to Brooklyn when he first came into the majors and never left it, even after the Dodgers shifted to Los Angeles. He was very near the end of his active playing career, but the Mets picked him up in the expansion draft because of his tremendous popularity in New York. Besides, in common with most aging sluggers, he could still hit. He proved it in the opening game at St. Louis, where he smashed one out of the park.

When the Mets opened at the Polo Grounds, the fans began calling for him even before the lineup was announced. I was standing at the microphone on the field, with Coach Solly Hemus beside me. When it was time to introduce the starting ballplayers, I read the batting order, which I had taken off the dugout wall. It had Hodges' name on it.

"At first base," I said, "Gil Hodges, number fourteen."

There was a tremendous roar from the crowd, which choked off into a chorus of boos as Jim Marshall ran out. At the same moment, Hemus dug his elbow into my ribs and whispered, "Marshall, Marshall." After infield practice, Hodges reported he had pulled a muscle and Casey had taken him out of the lineup.

I hastily announced, "At first base, Jim Marshall," but that only made the boos louder. And all through the game Marshall received the same treatment whenever he made a move. Later, with good reason, he moaned, "What kind of a New York start was that? Without doing a thing, I got booed just for not being Gil Hodges." He went to Japan at the end of the season, where he has played ball ever since. I don't blame him.

When the Dodgers came to town in July of 1962, Leo Durocher, then one of their coaches, went to the locker room for some penicillin to ward off a cold. It gave him an immediate and terrifying reaction, so bad that the public-address announcer called for a doctor. Although it was a couple of hours before the game, there happened to be one in the stands. After giving Durocher emergency treatment, he sent Leo to the hospital in an ambulance.

Word spread around the ball park that Durocher was desperately ill, but Tom Meany learned on phoning the hospital that he had pulled out of it very well. At about this time ceremonies honoring Gil Hodges began at home plate. Abe Stark, who had been closely identified with the Dodgers in Brooklyn, stepped to the microphone and in a voice quivering with emotion asked the fans to stand in a moment of silence and prayer for the good health and well-being of Leo Durocher.

"A fine thing," Meany whispered to me. "They're all standing reverently praying for the health of a guy who right this minute is probably sitting on the edge of his bed playing gin rummy."

The Mets, always trying but rarely getting anywhere, won only 40 games while losing 120 in their first year. When they went south in 1963 everybody had hopes that things would be better, and the New York writers sent optimistic stories to their papers back home. The opening game of the season, against St. Louis, was at the Polo Grounds. The Cardinal lead-off man hit a dinky dribbler down the third-base line and Charley Neal tore in for it. He fielded it perfectly, then threw it into right field. That was the first play of the 1963 season.

The Mets got two hits and were shut out. After the game I met Barney Kremenko of the New York *Journal American* in the press room. We looked at each other for a minute; then he said, "But in Florida they were better."

Of course they were. Only at home they were worse and in San Francisco much worse. Candlestick Park is very windy, and the Mets find the place most baffling. One afternoon Rod Kanehl, playing third base, went after a pop fly that seemed headed for short left field. He ran out and turned, just in time to see the ball land on the first-base side of the pitcher's mound.

Another time, Larry Burright was at short and Duke Snider in left when somebody popped up in that general direction. They almost ran into each other going after the ball before Snider realized where it was going. He stopped and pointed to the base line between second and first. It dropped there safely, proving that Burright and Snider weren't the only Mets who didn't know where it would land. Nobody else could catch it either.

When somebody complained to Stengel about the Candlestick Park wind, he shrugged and said, "It don't bother Willie Mays."

The ballplayers weren't the only people in the Met party who had trouble in San Francisco. One night the Union League Club had a dinner for Casey. Because the hall wasn't big enough for all the writers and radio personnel traveling with the team, it was decided to invite one writer and one radio man to represent everyone. I was designated as the radio man.

Casey, who had been in Stockton during the day, arrived late, giving everyone plenty of time to partake of the liquid refreshment available. The dais was on a raised stage, framed by a curtain. When we sat down to eat, I noticed the writer was missing, but he wasn't missing long. Lost behind the curtain, he tried to lean against it. He fell with a crash, tearing down an American flag on a pole beside him and landing with it draped around his shoulders. The result was a touching tableau, faintly reminiscent of the "Spirit of '76."

The year before the Mets came into existence, Roger Maris broke Babe Ruth's record when he hit 61 home runs. The next year Maris hit 33 to lead the Yankees, but Frank Thomas of the Mets hit 34. That made Thomas the home-run champion of New York and a member of the Met hall of fame for 1962. I mention this comforting statistic only to show how a typical Met hero is made. It was, of course, a straw that every good Met fan clutched gratefully that first year.

But the hero of heroes, the man of the moment, the "big guy" of the ball club was not a home-run hitter, a monosyllabic catcher, a Yale graduate, a couple of guys named Bob Miller, an old Dodger favorite, or a careless sports writer, but a first baseman so charmingly clumsy that he already belongs to baseball's ages. As long as there is a Met fan left to worship a Met hero, 1962 will be remembered as the year of Marvelous Marv Throneberry.

Throneberry was the worst regular first baseman in the major leagues, and if you don't believe me you could look it up, as Casey would say. His fielding average of .981 was the lowest. The only thing in which he led the National League was errors. He and Dick Stuart of the Pirates each had 17, but Stuart played in more games. Besides, Stuart was a consistent slugger. Throneberry was only an occasional one.

I don't know this for a fact, but I have a strong suspicion that the man who named him Marvelous Marv was Richie Ashburn, now a Phillies announcer but then in the twilight of a brilliant career. (The brilliant career of every Met was in its twilight.) Ashburn was Marv's straight man, cheering his every move, feeding him his lines, and nursing him through impromptu locker-room interviews.

One day, soon after Marv came to the Mets, his name was gone from his locker, replaced by a card that read Marvelous Marv. This must have been Ashburn's inspiration, although Richie never admitted it. In any event, the writers immediately picked up the name, we used it on the air, and before you could say Marvelous Marv the fans had adopted it.

Throneberry, a tall good-natured Tennesseean of twenty-eight, had been in and out of the majors for years when the Mets bought him from the Baltimore Orioles in May of 1962. He had spent seven seasons in the Yankees' system, and actually was with them—under Casey—for two. He had one notable claim to fame as a Yankee. He was one of four ballplayers they sent to Kansas City in the deal which brought them Roger Maris.

Once a minor-league slugger of great promise (he hit 42 home runs at Denver one year and 40 the next), Throneberry always found fielding a puzzle. He had played first base and the outfield with equal futility, but Casey put him on first base because nobody else could do any better. Although it would have been difficult to find anyone who could do much worse, it was an inspired move, for Throneberry, besides being almost wistfully inept, was a truly delightful young man.

His mistakes were not ordinary mistakes, nor did they come at ordinary times. Marvelous Marv saved the worst of them for the best of occasions. He inspired fans from bleachers to box seats to slap their foreheads in frustration while laughing with tears in their eyes. He was a genius at turning victory into defeat, a puller of boners, a wondrously bad judge of which base to throw to, a juggler of grounders, and a dropper of pop flies. He was not simply a Met; he was the Mets.

He didn't mean to be funny, which, I suppose, was what

made him so. He worked hard, never loafed, never gave up. He did the best he could. They only trouble with Marvelous Marv was, his best was none too good.

Met fans soon were addressing the bulk of their attention to him. They broke out signs reading, "Come on, Marv," "Marvelous Marv, we love you," "Let's get 'em, Marv," and "Marvelous Marv, you're our boy." His very appearance on the field was the signal for wild cheers. All he had to do to create excitement or set off gales of laughter was be there.

Everybody yelled encouragement, knowing it would do no good. Everybody exhorted him to heights which, for Throneberry, were impossible. Everybody begged him to "Go get 'em," knowing he wasn't going to go get 'em. But that didn't make any difference. The simple sight of Marvelous Marv was, to a true Met fan, worth the price of admission.

One day I looked down from the booth and saw a group of youngsters with T shirts spelling out M-A-R-V. Marvelous Marv T shirts came out and were bought by the thousands. We used to see them all over the ballpark. Kids came out with wide banners that read: "Cranberry, strawberry, we love Throneberry." The man was a legend before his time.

Earnest and friendly, he was always trying to explain why he did things the way he did. On an airplane riding west after a game the Mets blew when Marv let a grounder go through his legs, he sat down beside me and said, "Y'know, Lindsey, the trouble with me is I played in the outfield too much at Kansas City and Baltimore. You play ground balls differently in the outfield than you do at first base."

I had to agree that Marv certainly played ground balls differently, at first base, in the outfield, or anywhere else. Every time one was hit at him, it was even money and take your pick whether he would get it or not.

While fielding lapses were Marv's specialty, he didn't confine himself to them. One memorable afternoon, in a game against the Cubs at the Polo Grounds, he belted a ball deep into the right-field corner. By the time it was relayed back in to the infield, Marv was on third base. The crowd, which appreciated his good deeds as well as his mistakes, was in ecstasy.

But Ernie Banks, the Cub first baseman, called for the ball, and when he stepped on the bag the umpire called Throneberry out. Marv had missed first on his way around the bases. Casey Stengel tore out of the dugout, and from where we were sitting it looked as if he were going to charge the umpire. He was waving his fists and yelling and dancing around like a man possessed.

When he reached first base, still arguing and gesticulating, Cookie Lavagetto, the first-base coach, said something and Casey suddenly calmed down. He continued to talk to the umpire, but now his appeal was obviously perfunctory, and he soon slowly began making his way back to the dugout.

In the dressing room later, I asked Lavagetto what he had told Casey.

"All I said," Cookie replied, "was, 'Skipper, don't argue too long. He missed second base too.'"

Stengel's birthday was in late July, and there was a big celebration, complete with cake. About six weeks later, Marv also had a birthday, but it was ignored. He grumbled to Casey that nobody had thought to give him a cake. Casey scratched his chin, looked at him a moment, and said, "Well, we was going to get you one, but we figured you'd drop it."

That winter the New York baseball writers gave Throneberry the annual good guy award in memory of Ben Epstein, noting in the citation that he had taken a fantastic amount of good-natured ribbing in the best of grace. In the spring of 1963 he was a holdout, prompting George Weiss to say, "Marv got the good guy award mixed up with the most valuable player award."

Throneberry finally got his salary problems straightened out and began the 1963 season with the Mets. But by that time

Casey had other plans for first base. It wasn't long before Marv was farmed out to Buffalo, and soon after that he retired from baseball.

One day in 1965, when it was my turn to do a pre-game radio show, in which I alternated with Bob Murphy over station WHN, I had a call from the station to go to a certain room in a midtown hotel to interview a mystery guest who would appear at Shea Stadium that night, playing for the station in a game between the WHN personnel and the New York writers before the Mets game. I went to the room, and there, clad in slacks and an undershirt, was Marvelous Marv. That night, when he came to bat as a pinch-hitter for the WHN team, he brought down the house. Met fans never forget, nor will Met heroes ever die.

Chapter 12

"Whatsamatta Widda Mets?"

HOW do you describe a Met fan? Once, in a television interview, I asked Casey Stengel to do it for me. Here is what he said:

"I wanna say that the Mets fans has been marvelous. And they come out and done better than we have on the field and I'm glad we got 'em. If we could do as well as them it'd be better and we're tryin' 'cause in supportin' us the attendance has got trimmed. You'd think we'd do better and without all these people turnin' out to help us we wouldn't but they come out with the banners and the cheers and it's 'Metsie, Metsie, Metsie.' When the little children first start to speak they once said, 'Mamma' and 'Papa' but with the fans we got they say the first thing 'Metsie, Metsie, Metsie.' I'm glad to see that we got so many of the ladies turnin' out to see our team 'cause it proves that we got effeminate appeal which is the result of my charm school which I run as chief instructor in effeminate appeal and we got 'em turnin' out with their dates, the young 'uns and the old 'uns, and I wish we could do it better on the field. And you might wanna say wasn't it the World's Fair that drew the people into the park and I'd hafta say no maybe it was we helped out Mr. Moses and his fair across the street because if you'll remember we drew over a million people at the Polo Grounds which was fallin' in and they didn't have no fair acrost the street and you couldn't park it, unless you drove on the subway and there's no place to dine."

One June afternoon I walked around midtown Manhattan on a few errands. The traffic cop at the corner of Fifth Avenue and 57th Street yelled, "Hey, Lindsey, when we gonna start winnin' a few?"

Halfway down the block a doorman stopped me. "Y'think the Mets'll do it tonight?" he asked.

Two little boys carrying shoeshine boxes brushed by me. They stopped, looked around, and one cried, "Hey, Lindsey, whatsamatta widda Mets?"

I passed a newsdealer, who said from behind his papers, "Ain't they *ever* gonna win?"

When I came to a peddler selling hot dogs at the curb, he grunted: "Them Mets!"

The Mets were for the common people, I thought—the policemen and the doormen and the shoeshine boys and the newsdealers and the hot-dog peddlers. I headed for the Morgan Guaranty Trust on Madison Avenue to cash a check.

The Morgan Guaranty Trust is not a place where people fool around with bugles and banners and Bronx bazoos and all the other equipment peculiar to Met fans. It always scares me a little, for everything there is very prim and proper. When I first came to New York I had so much trouble identifying myself it took a year before any of the cashiers recognized me as a steady customer. When I walk into the Morgan Guaranty Trust I tread lightly and speak softly. I never expect to meet Met fans there.

I cashed my check and started out. Just before I reached the exit, a man at one of the huge mahogany desks behind a railing softly—and I thought rather ominously—asked, "Mr. Nelson, may I talk to you a minute?"

I wondered what I had done. Was my account overdrawn? Had a check bounced? Had they decided after all these years to stop letting me do business with them? Was something wrong with my identification? Had something happened to my credit?

I stepped to the other side of the railing, feeling like a school kid walking into the principal's office. The man invited me to a chair and said, "Mr. Nelson, we have a depositor with whom we are frequently in touch, a lady on Long Island. The other day she called with a question I couldn't answer. Perhaps you can."

"I'll try," I said.

"Is Ron Swoboda Polish, Czech, Russian, or what?" he asked.

I walked down Madison to 51st Street and stepped into a little lunch counter for a cup of coffee. The fellow who runs it is very heavy, very cold, and very impersonal. I've wandered in and out of the place from time to time for years, without ever seeing him smile or getting more out of him than a grunt.

He poured me some coffee and went about his business. When I finished he was at the other end of the counter, and I couldn't get his attention to pay the check. Finally I got off my stool and yelled, "May I have my check for the coffee?"

The counter man turned, spread out his arms, palms up, grinned, and said, "No charge to the Metsies."

That night I went to Shea Stadium, where I watched Carl Willey of the Mets pitch eight great innings against his old club, the Milwaukee Braves. With a one-run lead going into the ninth, all he had to do to win was get three men out. He got two, but filled the bases in the process and was obviously very tired. Casey Stengel pulled him out and sent in Galen Cisco.

Cisco walked the first batter he faced, and the tying run came in. He hit the second batter, and that scored the winning run.

Murph and I waited for Ralph to finish his post-game show, and the three of us went down to the Half Note in Greenwich Village for a late snack and a chance to get away from thoughts of batters walking and being hit and runners trooping across the plate. As we listened to a jazz combo and waited for our food, the chef, waving his arms like a sea gull, came through the kitchen door and stood at our table.

"What happened?" he screamed. "I haven't got a radio in the kitchen, so I parked my car on the street outside the kitchen door. All night long, I'm cookin' and runnin' out the door to turn on the car radio and check the Mets—back and forth, back and forth. It's goin' great. Willey's got 'em, and the Mets are still in front. I gotta come back to the kitchen, but I rush out and slide into the car seat and turn on the radio, and the Braves have the bases loaded up. Willey's out of the game and Cisco walks one and hits one and we lose it."

He stopped waving his arms long enough to hit his forehead with the heel of one hand and yelled over the noise of the jazz combo, "I can't believe it. We had it won and now we lose. I sit there a minute because I'm in shock. Now, I remember the kitchen and I rush back. I got a pan full of spaghetti on the stove. The spaghetti is burned and the bottom of the pan is burned and the Mets lose a ball game on account of Cisco can't get the ball over the plate. What happened?"

On June 1, 1965, Governor Nelson Rockefeller of New York signed a bill abolishing capital punishment for all but two narrowly limited types of cases. This meant commutation of sentence for most of the twenty men in Sing Sing's death row.

How did they take it? When newspapermen asked Warden Wilfred L. Denno, he replied, "There was no reaction at all. They just kept listening to the ball game." It was the Met game they were listening to. And that day the Mets walloped the Cubs, 10–5, for their second victory in two days.

When the Mets played an exhibition game with the Yankees for the first Mayor's Trophy in 1963, a crowd of 50,000 people jammed Yankee Stadium. Most of them were Met fans. During the early part of batting practice even the ushers cheered madly as each Met came up.

While the Yankees were warming up, Whitey Ford sneaked up behind Elston Howard, cupped his hands, and yelled in Howard's ear, "You couldn't carry Choo Choo Coleman's glove." When the startled Howard looked around, Ford said, "Just thought I'd get you used to what you're going to hear all night tonight."

Everybody was kidding and laughing and having such a wonderful time that you would have sworn nobody cared whether the Mets won or lost. But one man cared very much indeed. Casey Stengel wanted this ball game as much as he had ever wanted anything in his life, including all the World Series games the Yankees played when he was their manager.

An exhibition game in mid-season is usually shared by several pitchers so nobody will miss a regular turn in the pennant race. Stengel decided to start Jay Hook and have someone else finish. Hook pitched five excellent innings, and when he was through Casey called the bullpen.

"Who ya got ready, Mr. Weiss?" he asked Ernie White, the pitching coach. He always called White "Mr. Weiss."

"Ken MacKenzie's throwing," White said.

"Mr. Weiss," Casey said, "ain't we got somebody better than that?"

"Carl Willey?"

"Heat 'im up, Mr. Weiss."

Willey pitched four shutout innings, and the Mets won.

I've seen hundreds of more important sports events and many bigger crowds. I know how crazy New York went when Bobby Thomson hit his dream home run to win the 1951 pennant and how wild Milwaukee was when the 1957 Braves won the world's championship and how Brooklyn celebrated when the Dodgers won pennants and the 1955 world's championship before going to Los Angeles.

What happened in the Bronx that night when the Mets beat the Yankees in an exhibition game must have compared favorably to all the other great victory demonstrations of baseball history. Horns tooted, firecrackers popped, hats flew, bugles blew, bells rang, and people danced up and down the aisles, cheering, laughing, shaking hands, and whacking each other on the back. Only a phalanx of ushers and policemen guarding the diamond kept them from overflowing to the field and snake-dancing around there. If there had been goal posts, they would have come down faster than you could say "Mets."

I stayed around the ball park nearly an hour before going out to get my car. The parking lot was still half full of screaming Met fans yelling congratulations back and forth. After I got out of there, the only thing I could think of was the ticker-tape parade the Mets were given down Broadway when they first went to New York. Traffic was at a standstill as people leaned out of windows, yelling and tooting horns and adding to the confusion on the street. It was one of the wildest sports nights I've ever seen, one of the slowest rides I've ever had. It took nearly two hours to reach the Triborough Bridge, and not until I crossed it did life return to normal. I heard later that the Bronx never really did get to bed that night.

Leonard Koppett of *The New York Times* appeared at the Mets game at the Polo Grounds the next night and handed us a typewritten sheet with the lyrics of a song that was the hit of the annual New York baseball writers' dinner and show the following January. He had dashed it off in a moment of inspiration. Sung to the tune of "The Battle Hymn of the Republic," it began:

These eyes have seen the glory of the Yankees in defeat.
They ain't even champions of 157th Street.

And the refrain went: "Glory, glory, Casey Stengel."

It takes very little to get a Met fan started on something new. In 1965 we were in Philadelphia on my birthday, May 25. As the game began, a telegram was delivered to me in the radio booth. I shoved it in my pocket, figuring I'd look at it later. While I was working, Joe Gallagher reached for it and handed it to Ralph Kiner. When it was Ralph's turn to take over, he read it on the air. It came from Hollywood and it said, "Dear Lindsey, so sorry I can't be there to share your birthday with you as we have done so many times in the past. Signed, Gloria Swanson." It had been sent as a gag by Irv Kaze, the public-relations director of the Los Angeles Angels.

Pretty soon other wires began pouring in. I don't know how many I received, but most of them were signed by prominent people, everyone from Ted Lewis to Teddy Roosevelt. To this day I don't know who actually sent them. All I know is they were Met fans listening to the game that night.

We have the Associated Press with us—at least they listen to our games. On the last day of the 1965 season, Jack Lang of the Long Island *Press* announced on the public-address system, "The Associated Press reports that Don Heffner will be the manager of the Cincinnati Reds."

I relayed the message to the television audience, adding that this was an unconfirmed wire-service report. "It would only be fair to say," I went on, "that in recent years the Associated Press has reported some managerial appointments that never quite came off."

A couple of minutes later, the AP machine in the press box

sent me a message reading: "The Associated Press has more subscribers than any other wire service. We must be doing something right."

Met fans—they're all over the place. Before going to St. Petersburg for spring training in 1965, I took my wife, Mickie, on a Caribbean cruise. When we arrived in the Virgin Islands we hired a taxi for a guided tour of Charlotte Amalie in St. Thomas. After showing us around, the driver pulled up in front of the ball park.

"Did you ever hear of the New York Mets?" he asked.

"Oh, yes," I said, "I've heard of the New York Mets."

"You ever hear of Joe Christopher?"

"Yes, I've heard of Joe Christopher."

"Well," he said, "this is where Joe Christopher played as a little-bitty boy."

So when Joe Christopher was with the Mets the ball park where he played had become an item on the conventional guided tour of Charlotte Amalie.

John Steinbeck is a Met fan. Here is what he wrote in a 1965 magazine piece:

In baseball I like the audience almost better than the game. I guess that is why I am a Met fan. My wife was a Dodger fan. . . . This, of course, was before they defected to the West. Any kind of skulduggery and ineptness my wife could forgive and even defend, but treason she could not take. She is a Met fan now, and our house is whole again.

Early on, to save arguments, I became an Oriole fan and even bought a little stock in that club. If you were for anyone else you got an argument, but if you said you were an Oriole fan people just laughed and let you alone. I thought I had a guarantee that they would stay on the bottom, but now they have double-crossed me by climbing up. I nearly went to the Senators, because there is a federal law which forbids them to win. Then the Mets happened, and I was stuck.

Before the 1965 season began, the Mets signed two prominent coaches, Yogi Berra and Warren Spahn. Berra had just been fired after a year as manager of the Yankees, during which he led them to a pennant. Spahn had been dropped by the Braves, with whom he had become one of the great southpaw pitchers of all time. Both were originally listed as player-coaches and actually served as a battery once in an exhibition game in Florida. Berra was used as a pinch-hitter a few times in the regular season before asking retirement as an active player.

In accordance with baseball law, he was put on waivers at a price of one dollar. If unclaimed, he could then go on the inactive list and become just a coach. When his name was released on the waiver list, a woman wrote the Mets, enclosing a dollar, and asked that her Yogi Bear be sent to the address she gave. The Mets replied with a deadpan explanation that it was a Berra, not a Bear, they were making available. Another woman wrote asking to buy Yogi for a dollar. We invited her to Shea Stadium and put her on Ralph's pre-game television show.

After the all-star break, one-dollar waivers were asked on Warren Spahn for the purpose of giving him his unconditional release. The Mets got a letter from a man who enclosed a one-dollar money order. He asked to buy Spahn, then added, "I would also like some advice. Will you please inform me what the baseball procedure is concerning what I do in case I want to get rid of him?"

A thirteen-year-old boy also sent a letter with a dollar in it and the information that he would like to claim Spahn for his sandlot team, but only as a conditional purchase. He said he wanted to look at Spahn before closing the deal, and asked that the dollar be returned in case he changed his mind. Later in the same letter he waxed a bit more enthusiastic, and ended by saying, "On second thought, I'll take him sight unseen."

In 1964 the producers of the television show "Candid Camera," decided to do a baseball sequence. They rigged up a fake television set with a very thin piece of paper for a screen, on which a film showed pictures of Mets games. People coming in would stare at the screen and at the proper time would see a ball apparently coming right into the camera. It would burst through the paper and land in their laps, while their reactions were recorded for the show. I was in a back room with a microphone, doing the commentary.

In most cases the people were fascinated at the sight of the ball and completely startled when it came right out of the camera and landed on them. But one man didn't flinch at all. He looked up, fingered the ball, and said, "Well, it's the Mets. You can expect anything."

Met fans come in all ages. One Met Banner Day in 1965 a small boy with a crew cut carried a banner that said:

> Aw, gee, don't get sore,
> The Mets and I are only four.

Another banner said: "The rest of the league is just lucky." One of the winning banners proclaimed:

> To err is human,
> To forgive is a Mets fan.

Even the ballplayers got into the act that day. They poured out of the dugout unrolling a huge streamer that read:

> From all of us, and Casey too,
> We really think the world of you.

One day I was late getting up to the booth because I had to MC something from the field. As I hurried in I brushed by an old man with a huge beard, accompanied by a youngster.

The two were talking to Ralph, who had just had them on his show. I paid no attention and got settled in the television booth, then heard Ralph say, "Bing, you know Lindsey."

I turned around. It was Bing Crosby, made up for the movie *Stagecoach*, and his young son. They had dropped in at Shea Stadium to see the Mets on their way to the airport. Crosby and Ralph had been friends for many years. On Ralph's show, Crosby, explaining his shaggy appearance, said he was playing the part of a bibulous character. Later, on our way out of the stadium after the game was over, a woman stopped Ralph and said, "I saw your show before the game and I wish I could meet Mr. Crosby. I heard him say he was playing a bibulous character. I'm very much interested in the Bible and would like to know what character he was playing."

Chapter 13

The
Two-Buck
Speech

CASEY STENGEL is inexhaustible. He not only outlasted everyone at night, but he beat practically everyone up in the morning without looking in the least the worse for wear. Men young enough to be his grandsons wandered into coffee shops for breakfast puffy-eyed and morose after a large evening, but Casey was always neat and cheerful.

The slightest excuse was an occasion for a party with Casey, and if he couldn't find an excuse he was likely to throw one anyhow. One of the big events of the year was his birthday. Whenever Casey had one, there was a huge blast attended by all nonplaying personnel who could claim any connection, distant or close, with the Mets.

The Mets themselves began Casey's seventy-third birthday celebration in 1963 by beating the Cardinals in St. Louis. This

142

made it a double occasion for a party, because the Mets rarely beat the Cardinals anywhere. The game ended around eleven-thirty at night, so the party at the Chase-Park Plaza didn't get underway until after midnight.

It went on and on and on. I quit at about two-thirty and went to bed. I'm usually up early, and I met a writer on the elevator who had outlasted me the night before.

"How long did it go on?" I asked.

"I left at four and it was still going," he said.

"You mean Casey was still up then?"

"He was just getting started."

We were just getting started on our breakfast when Casey, freshly shaved and dressed to the nines, came bouncing in. After he joined us, the waitress brought over a menu. He looked at it briefly, then looked up at her, and said, "The Cardinals don't seem to be winnin' much lately. What seems to be your trouble?"

The Dodgers were at Shea Stadium for Casey's seventy-fourth birthday. That time we had a celebration right on the field before the game. Of all the gifts he received, one gave him particular pleasure. Al Moore of the Rheingold Brewery had gone over to the Polo Grounds, then being demolished, and bought a set of four grandstand seats from the approximate site where Casey and Edna had met back in 1923. Al had the seats painted, and the presentation to Casey was made right on the field. He and Edna sat down on them and, while the cameras clicked, he reached over and kissed her. Those four old Polo Grounds seats are now beside the Stengels' pool at their home in Glendale, California.

Casey's seventy-fifth birthday in 1965 was like a Polish wedding: the celebrations were scheduled to go on for a week. Casey would be seventy-five on July 30, but the Mets were playing in Philadelphia that night, and everyone wanted a special celebration in New York. The club decided to observe the occasion at Shea Stadium on Sunday, July 25, the last day before Casey's birthday that the team would be in town. And Mayor Robert F. Wagner of New York, who wanted to honor Casey on a weekday so the whole town could participate, proclaimed Friday, July 23, Casey Stengel Day.

The Mets beat the Pirates in Pittsburgh the night before, and then flew to Buffalo for an exhibition game against their International League farm team. While the rest of the party went along, Ralph Kiner, Bob Murphy, and I, who didn't have to broadcast the game, flew to New York with Casey. On the plane he said, "Well, I'm gonna be down there tomorrow and the mayor's gonna do something nice for me and what am I supposed to say? Do I thank him or the people of New York or who?"

Finally he turned to me and said, "You wanna make some money?"

"Not particularly," I said, wondering what the gag was.

"I'm gonna give you two bucks to write me a speech to say when I get that scroll from the mayor, 'cause I don't wanna go down there and get everything all bollixed up," Casey said.

"Okay," I said. "I'll give you a two-buck speech. When the mayor gives you the scroll, you just step up to the microphone and say, 'Thank you very much.'"

Casey frowned. "Just 'Thank you very much'?" he said.

"That's all."

I spent the next day at home on Long Island. At about three in the afternoon somebody at NBC phoned and said, "Did you know Casey Stengel just announced his retirement?"

"What?"

"At City Hall when the mayor gave him that scroll," the NBC man said, "he accepted it by announcing his retirement."

"Casey didn't announce his retirement," I said. "What he did was bollix up his speech."

"Well, all the late editions of the afternoon papers are leading with the story."

Sure enough, that afternoon there were headlines in every paper in town that Casey had announced his retirement. Of course he hadn't. Heaven only knows what he did announce, for I'm sure he delivered a lengthy, confusing speech, during which he might have said almost anything. The quote which sounded to his listeners like a retirement announcement was, "When I go home this fall, I hope to leave a young team."

City Hall was covered by fellows who weren't baseball writers and had never been around Casey before. They made the mistake of taking literally what Casey meant to be his typical "filler" material. That night he told the New York writers in Buffalo, where he went right after accepting the mayor's scroll, "I've been going home to California for a long time, but I'm still active, ain't I? What they interpret ain't in my mind. It's in theirs. I can't help that."

Then he added, "I didn't go to City Hall to retire. The mayor's retirin' and I'm not competin' with him. I went to City Hall to get a scroll. Also to hear the mayor proclaim Casey Stengel Day. I never had a day before."

Casey spent the next twenty-four hours denying his retirement, while assuring everyone that the first people to know it when he did retire would be George Weiss and the Mets, not Mayor Wagner and the reporters who covered New York's City Hall. By the time I saw him again, Casey was sick and tired of telling people he didn't mean what everybody had thought he had meant.

He didn't greet me with a handshake, a hello, or anything else. All he said was, "I shoulda bought your two-buck speech."

I guess the Mets wished he had bought a two-buck speech one day in 1963 after Ron Hunt, then a twenty-two-year-old rookie, won a game with a late-inning base hit. Casey was always ten feet off the ground after the Mets won. When this one ended he said on television, "It's young ballplayers like Ron Hunt that have a great chance with the New York Mets, and if you're anybody who wants to play baseball, you want to get to the major leagues in a hurry, just sign up with the New York Mets because the New York Mets can get you to the major leagues quicker than anybody else, and if there's anybody out there lookin' in on the television that thinks they can play baseball in the major leagues, get in touch with the New York Mets."

In five minutes it seemed as if everybody in New York who had ever had a baseball glove in his hand wanted a job with the Mets. The switchboard at the Polo Grounds lit up like a Christmas tree. The ball club had to keep a special crew of telephone operators on duty until things quieted down, which wasn't until well after midnight.

Sometimes people wondered whether Casey really ran the team. There were rumors that others made the decisions, that Casey was really nothing more than window dressing, and even that he nodded off to sleep on the bench during games. There was no truth whatever to any of this. When Casey managed the Mets he was the boss of everything that happened on the field.

When the Mets went to Pompano Beach, Florida, for a spring exhibition game with the Senators one day, Casey got tied up in a meeting and didn't go in the team bus. Coaches Solly Hemus and Cookie Lavagetto ran pre-game practice. I waited around for the lineup, but they couldn't help. Neither could anyone else. Everything stood still because Casey wasn't there. Five minutes before the game a cab came screeching up behind the grandstand and Casey, in street clothes, jumped out. He ran to the bench and made out the lineup, and not until then did we know who was playing for the Mets that day.

You could always depend on Casey for a classic comment on any baseball subject. When the Astrodome opened in 1965, the glare from the sun on the roof made fly balls so difficult to catch that eventually the roof had to be painted. Before the Mets went in there for the first time, someone remarked to Casey, "They're dropping a lot of fly balls in the Astrodome."

"We can do that outdoors," he replied.

"Are you going to work on fly balls?" he was asked.

"They don't bother us none," he said. "We're still workin' on grounders."

After nearly two years in the Polo Grounds, the Mets began to find the range of those short left- and right-field foul lines. One night they hit two Chinese homers which dropped into the lower deck of the grandstand less than 260 feet from the plate. When the game ended, Casey said, "Just when my fellows learn to hit in this ball park, they're gonna tear it down."

As he had with the Yankees in his days of glory, Casey was always writing and rewriting lineups, batting orders, and team rosters, especially in the spring, when he had to decide which men to keep and which to cut. Shortly before we left St. Petersburg in 1964, he came out of his suite late one evening looking perplexed.

When I asked him what was wrong, he said, "I been back there cuttin' the squad. And every time we cut somebody, we're weaker."

Casey never tried to blame anyone else for his own mistakes. One night Carl Willey had a 2–0 lead going into the ninth, then began to weaken. The Braves got a couple of men on, and Casey called the bullpen to see who was warming up. He decided to stick with Willey. The next thing he knew, the Braves had the game tied up with men still on base. Casey hastily called the bullpen again, but as Ernie White answered the phone the winning run came in.

"Mr. Weiss," Casey said, "we just blew the ball game."

I was on the announcing crew that did the broadcast the day Casey captivated President John F. Kennedy at the all-star game in Washington in 1962. Casey was a coach for the National League team, which Fred Hutchinson of the Reds managed that year. The President sent word to the dugout that he'd like to see Casey between innings. Casey came up, removed his cap, shook hands, began talking, then suddenly excused himself.

Pointing to Hutch, he said, "Mr. President, I'd love to stay here and talk to you and if I was workin' for myself today I would, but I'm workin' for that other feller so I got to get back to my business."

Casey was one of the few men I ever knew who succeeded in changing that most inflexible of literary endeavors, the wording of a radio commercial. Somehow or other he became involved in a contract to do a couple of brief ones for Arpège perfume. The copy was very simple. All he had to say was, "This is Casey Stengel. Promise her anything—but give her Arpège, by Lanvin."

He had several runs at it and made it faultlessly to the last word, but the French pronunciation of Lanvin kept throwing him. Finally the agency decided to let it go Casey's way. His commercials came out in two versions. One read: "This is Casey Stengel. Promise her anything—but give her Arpège, by Levi." The other went: "Promise her anything—give her Arpège, by Levine."

Casey was such a master of the ad lib that even professional entertainers were well advised not to tangle with him. One night the comic on the bill at the Edgewater Beach Hotel in Chicago spotted us in the back of the room and started introducing Casey, who was right in the middle of dinner. Casey stood up, took a bow, and sat down, but the comic wouldn't let him alone. He kept calling attention to Casey with corny remarks. When Casey tried to ignore him, the comic finally said, "Say, Casey, that Shea Stadium in New York is a fantastic place, brand new, with all the latest improvements. Tell us about it."

Casey stood up and said, "Yes, it is. As a matter of fact, it has fifty-five rest rooms and I'm gonna go out and use one right now." And with that he went through the door.

One day in the spring of 1965 I asked Casey in the clubhouse at Huggins-Stengel Field in St. Petersburg about Bud Harrelson, a rookie shortstop who was expected to get out of the Army any moment.

"Well, now, I wanna tell ya about that," Casey said. "He's in the Army and you don't mess around with them people. As for myself, you might know I was in the Navy in the First war, and I was with some people that we guarded the Gowanus Canal and not a single submarine got into it. But he can field, and he can run, and if he can hit enough I don't know but you'd hafta say he's the first after McMillan that we got coming up for the future."

Casey talked about the future, knowing there wasn't much of it left for him, but I never heard him show serious concern about his age. Once he told me, "No one else in here is gettin' younger, and I'm the only one gettin' older." Another time, after a birthday, he remarked, "Some people my age get dead."

The possibility of retirement being always imminent because of his age, we wondered who, if anyone, Casey would like to see take his place. While he and I were having breakfast in the coffee shop of the Hotel Schroeder in Milwaukee in June of 1965, he suddenly began talking about Coach Wes Westrum.

"And I wanna tell ya," he said, "that he's there on the bench and he's got slick, now I don't mean smart-aleck slick like ballplayers tryin' to trim ya, but he's slick thinkin' and he's got some ideas and, yessir, he comes up with some moves."

At the time I didn't think much about it, for Casey often spoke of his coaches, all of whom he liked. A month later there was an old-timers' day at Shea Stadium. It was held on Saturday, July 24, the day after all the excitement over Casey's "retirement" announcement at City Hall. The old-timers' day theme that year was the rivalry between the New York Giants and the Brooklyn Dodgers, and the former ballplayers appeared in their old uniforms. Casey had played for both teams, but he wore a Dodger uniform that afternoon.

I was at the microphone on the field, introducing the former New York favorites. As each man appeared, he got his share of applause, but everyone was obviously waiting for Casey. Just as I was about to introduce him, a jet plane took off from La Guardia Airport nearby, and I had to hold back until it passed, since the noise drowned everything else out. When I finally could say, "Casey Stengel," and he ran out, he received a thunderous ovation.

Although another birthday party for him was scheduled for the next day, that was the last time Casey Stengel was ever introduced in uniform to a baseball crowd.

That night there was an old-timers' party at Toots Shor's. We were told to be there at seven-thirty, but when we arrived the only people around were waiters and writers. Everyone else had been told to get there at eight-thirty. Casey, still smarting from the excitement over his City Hall announcement two days before, looked around and said, "Well, since I retired I see I'm packin' 'em in."

There were soon plenty of people around, and by nine o'clock the party was going full tilt. As usual, it lasted longer than I felt like staying up. It was still at its height when I left to go home around midnight.

I arrived at Shea Stadium early the next morning. There was to be a doubleheader, and Casey's seventy-fifth birthday celebration was scheduled between games. While I was in the press room, Matt Winick, the club statistician, came over and whispered, "Harold [Harold Weissman, the public-relations director] is getting an announcement ready. Casey's in Roosevelt Hospital with a broken hip. Nobody seems to know how it happened."

Casey had spent the night at the home of Joe DeGregorio, comptroller of the Mets, because it was close to the ball park. He complained of such severe pains that DeGregorio sent for Gus Mauch, the Mets' trainer, who got over there at about three in the morning. Mauch called the club physician, Dr. Peter LaMotte, who ordered Casey to the hospital. He later said Casey must have broken his hip getting out of DeGregorio's car, since that was when he first felt the pain.

Before the game began that day, word came from the hospital that Casey wanted Westrum to run the team. Westrum finished the season as interim manager and later was named as Casey's successor.

During the weeks Casey spent in the hospital he received thousands of letters from fans all over the country. They were addressed many different ways, but they all seemed to reach him. Some simply said, "Casey Stengel, New York." He even got one addressed, "Man with the broken hip, New York City."

Before going home to California, Casey made one final appearance at Shea Stadium. There, as television, newsreel, and still cameras flashed, George Weiss held up Casey's uniform and said, "Casey, this uniform number thirty-seven will be retired. It will never again be worn by a member of the Met organization, but will be put under glass to be viewed by fans who come to Shea Stadium."

"I hope they don't put me under glass," Casey said.

In November of 1965 a group of writers and Met officials sitting around the manager's office at Shea Stadium decided to phone Casey at his home in Glendale, California.

"How's your hip coming along?" somebody asked him.

"Well, I wanna tell ya about that," Casey said. "It's pretty good and it ain't. I get maybe two good days and a bad one, or maybe three good days and a bad one. Now that ain't a bad percentage."

"Better," remarked Fred Trask, one of the Met owners, "than the ball club's."

Chapter 14

A
Met
Is a
Met

THE Mets didn't do any better as time went on
than they had before time went on. They finished
tenth in their first two years and tenth in their second two.
Each year the ballplayers were new, the heroes were new, the
crowd favorites were new, but the results were the same. There
was one significant difference between the later Mets and the
earlier Mets. The earlier Mets were hopeless. The later Mets
were promising. Young, earnest, hard-working, some had
touches that were much like talent.

During the winter baseball meetings at Fort Lauderdale in
November of 1965, George Weiss, thumbing through the *Base-
ball Register*, noticed that that very day, November 28, was
Wes Westrum's birthday. He thought it would be a good idea
to have a party for the new manager, so he told road secretary
Lou Niss to make arrangements.

The party was held in the penthouse restaurant of the Shera-ton Hotel. The food was good, the liquid refreshments were plentiful, and everybody had a wonderful time. The *pièce de résistance* was the birthday cake. The lights were dimmed, and in came a waiter bearing a beauty, complete with lighted candles. He set it down in front of Westrum, who was under-standably and appropriately moved.

Westrum took a deep breath and blew out the candles. The lights went on, and he stared at the inscription on the cake. It read: "Happy Birthday, Lou Niss."

Later the whole Met party moved on to the Fontainebleau Hotel in Miami Beach for the rest of the meetings and dis-covered there were no rooms available. The room clerk explained that the previous occupants were staying over a day and the management couldn't get them out. This prompted somebody to say, "Even at hotels the Mets can't get anybody out."

During the 1965 baseball season pitcher Jack Fisher used a Rambler when in New York. Rambler was the official Met car, and several were provided for the ball club. When the season ended and Fisher was getting ready to leave for home, Harold Weissman asked him how his golf game was.

"Good Lord," Fisher said. "I've got to call the Rambler people and see what they've done with that car. I left my golf clubs in the trunk."

In 1965 a fine young pitcher named Frank (Tug) McGraw joined the Mets. He had worked his way through college as a barber, and every so often somebody on the team asked him for a haircut when the club was on the road. Tug's big moment came one night at Shea Stadium when he beat Sandy Koufax of the Dodgers. Later I asked him if that was the greatest thrill of his life.

He thought a minute and said, "It was a big thrill, all right. But I think the biggest was the night Yogi Berra phoned my room and asked me to go up and give him a haircut."

Berra wouldn't ride the subway, but Rod Kanehl loved it. Yogi told me once why he didn't. "When I first came to New York," he said, "I lived at the Edison Hotel, and the doorman said it was easy to get to Yankee Stadium by subway, so I got on. At the first stop, I go shoved off the train onto the platform, people rushed by me, and I couldn't get back in. I never rode the subway again."

Kanehl was from Springfield, Missouri. The New York subway system fascinated him, and he spent most of his spare time on it. He used to ride up front with the motormen (they were all Met fans), and he went from one end of each of the various lines to the other. It didn't do him much good. He couldn't hit, and now he's the foremost authority on New York subways in Springfield, Missouri.

The Mets once had a pitcher named Bill Hunter. One night in 1964 they were leading the Dodgers by a run with two out in the last of the ninth and Maury Wills on third. Hunter got two strikes on the batter, and in the broadcasting booth we explained that he'd certainly work off a stretch instead of going into a windup because Wills was a threat to steal home with the tying run. To our amazement, Hunter dipped into a big windup while Wills streaked for the plate. Fortunately, Hunter's pitch was the third strike, which ended the game.

When we asked Hunter later why he used a windup, he said, "I'm not comfortable working off a stretch." If there's one thing relief pitchers must do, it's work off a stretch. They nearly always come into games with men on base who have to be held close. Hunter was probably the first relief pitcher in the history of modern baseball who wasn't comfortable working off a stretch. It was the greatest paradox I'd heard of since the doctor told golfer Cary Middlecoff he was allergic to grass.

Hunter's career ended abruptly in the middle of winter, qualifying him for all time as a true Met. He slipped on the ice and broke his collarbone.

In the spring of 1965 George Weiss got the great sprinter Jesse Owens to come to St. Petersburg and teach the Mets the fine points of running and quick starting. He was doing a wonderful job until he suffered a pinched nerve, a chronic condition which eventually necessitated an operation. It took the Mets only a week or ten days to slow down one of the world's fastest humans to a point where he could hardly drag himself across a room.

One of the most promising Met rookies of 1965 was an all-round athlete from Ryder College named Danny Napoleon. A hard-hitting right-handed outfielder, he had smashed 36 homers and batted .351 for Auburn in the New York–Pennsylvania League in 1964. He loved to tell the wonderfully weird story of one of those homers.

Late in the first game of a twi-night doubleheader, during that twilight period when artificial lights don't help but it's hard to see in natural light, Napoleon hit a tremendous wallop to left field. The last he saw of it, the ball was headed high over the fence, so he slowed down approaching second base, thinking he had a home run. To his amazement, the umpire called him out. When he began protesting, the umpire pointed to the left fielder, who came running in, waving the ball.

"He couldn't have reached it," Danny said. "That ball was headed for the next county."

By then Manager Clyde McCullough of the Auburn Mets was beside him, raising a terrible fuss. The whole Auburn team, in fact, was screaming and yelling at the umpire, but nobody was getting anywhere. Finally the umpire appealed to the opposing left fielder. "Did you really catch the ball?" he asked.

The outfielder started to say something, then grinned sheepishly. "The one Napoleon hit is going yet," he said. "I got this one out of my shirt."

The year at Auburn was Napoleon's first in organized baseball. He was so impressive in spring training that he made it all the way to the Mets in his second year.

One night Casey sent him up to pinch-hit in the ninth with two out, the bases full, and the Mets trailing the Giants by a run at Candlestick Park. On a two-strike count, Napoleon belted a screaming line drive to right center for a triple that cleared the bases, and the Mets won the ball game.

Everybody was so excited in the dugout that they practically danced their way out onto the field and up the runway leading from right field to the clubhouse. Clubhouse boys, trainers, coaches, players, and the batboy streamed out. They were all so happy they forgot the equipment. Only Casey was left. In a rosy sort of daze he gathered up some jackets, a bat or two, and a catcher's mask, and slowly followed the others.

As he approached the door of the Giant clubhouse, which the visitors must pass en route to their own at Candlestick Park, Casey, his arms still full, loudly started whistling the "Marseillaise." He poked his head in the door and yelled, "*Vive la France.*" When somebody in the Giant room remarked, "That Napoleon looks pretty good," Casey replied, "Not bad for a guy who keeps his hand stuck in his shirtfront all the time."

The first real star the Mets developed was Ron Hunt. He was only twenty-two years old when he reported at spring training in 1963, an intense, determined youth with four years of minor-league experience behind him. There seemed little chance that he would stick with the club, for he was a second baseman and there were two men ahead of him when he showed up at St. Pete. One was Larry Burright, who had started the previous season as the Dodger second baseman, the other Ted Schreiber, the Mets' number one draft choice. Schreiber was never a factor, and Burright, after a good start, quickly tailed off. After the Mets lost their first eight games in a row, Hunt went to second base. He made an immediate hit by doubling home the winning run against the Braves in the last of the ninth.

A reckless, fiery ballplayer who dove head first into bases on close plays, fought for every advantage, and never gave up, Hunt was soon the darling of the fans. He was a bit slow covering ground, but what he lacked in speed he made up for in spirit, and it wasn't long before he became one of the league's leading second basemen.

I suppose every Met must have his peculiarities, and Hunt was no exception. He was the possessor of such a wide variety of allergies that we sometimes wondered if he would make it to the ball park. He had hay fever all the year round, was subject to asthma attacks, got rashes, had to be careful what he ate, and carried the most awesome collection of pills I ever saw.

He was proud of being a big-leaguer, proud of being a Met, and proudest of all in 1964 when he was voted the National League's second baseman in the all-star game, which was at Shea Stadium that summer. I went to a press gathering the night before the game, with Al Moore of Rheingold, who lived on Long Island and had left his car in the Shea Stadium parking lot. After dinner we took the subway to the ball park, arriving there at about nine-thirty. Before going for his car, Moore had to pick up something inside the stadium, which was locked. We rang for the caretaker, and when he let us in he said, "Mr. Hunt just came through here."

"You mean he's here now?" I said.

"Yes, he's gone to the dugout.'"

While Al went up to get his package I walked through the runway to the dugout. There was Ron Hunt with his wife and a group of relatives who had come in from his home in Missouri for the all-star game. He was proudly showing them around. Except for the caretaker, they were the only people in the park.

Hunt was and is a ballplayers' ballplayer, a fighter with so much natural talent that any team in the majors would be glad to have him. He was the first Met to win the respect as well as the affection of the fans. He took baseball so seriously that everybody took him seriously. He was a star, not a character.

Ron Swoboda, on the other hand, may become both. When he appeared on the Met scene in 1965 he was already a character in the Marv Throneberry tradition, but without Throneberry's hopelessness. Throneberry, twenty-eight when he came to the Mets, had never made it big and never would. Nobody could have stopped him from making mistakes; nobody could have transformed him from an erratic, enthusiastic, earnest, well-meaning fumbler into a top-ranking major-league ballplayer.

Swoboda, only twenty years old in 1965, was also an erratic, enthusiastic, earnest, well-meaning fumbler, but with youth, promise, and talent. A six-foot-two-inch 200-pounder with tremendous power, he could develop into a slugging outfielder and a real star. Throneberry's mistakes came after ten years of intensive instruction in organized baseball. Swoboda's were the result of inexperience, for he had spent only a year in the minors.

No matter what happens to him, Swoboda has already left his imprint at Shea Stadium. In 1965 he was the most popular Met ballplayer since Throneberry, the great hero, the man of the moment. Throneberry was the Mets in the spirit of hopelessness that prevailed in 1962. Swoboda was the Mets in the spirit of promise that prevailed three years later, and will continue to prevail until they become a full-grown major-league ball club.

The first time I saw Swoboda was when he reported to the Mets fresh off the University of Maryland campus in the spring of 1964. He was a rawboned nineteen-year-old, and everything about him was big—his shoulders, his muscles, even his grin. He came up one day in batting practice and belted a ball over the center-field fence at Huggins-Stengel Field in St. Pete, a tremendous shot, well over 500 feet. No Mets and few Yankees (who trained there before the Mets) had ever done that.

Casey Stengel fell in love with the kid, whom he called "Soboda." A few days after Ron had hit his mammoth drive, George Altman slammed one high over the left-field fence. When Altman, an established major-league outfielder, came back to the dugout, Casey said, "Keep that up and you'll be another Soboda."

Swoboda started the 1964 season at Buffalo, where he played twenty-two games, but he wasn't ready for Triple A ball, so he spent the bulk of the year at Williamsport in the Eastern League. His manager there was Ernie White, the former Met pitching coach. Swoboda, back in St. Pete in the spring of 1965, continued to hit fantastically long belts, and just before the team broke camp he almost killed a photographer with a wild throw. The man never knew what hit him and had to be carried off the field on a stretcher.

On the way north we saw Ernie White in Charlotte, North Carolina. Out of baseball because of ill health, he had come over from his home to see the Mets. He took one look at Swoboda and asked, "How many people has he hurt so far?"

"He skulled a photographer in St. Pete the other day," I said.

"He'll skull a few more people before he's through," White said. "He's awkward and he doesn't know his own strength. He's the kind of kid who will turn around quickly in a bus and catch you in the eye with an elbow. Somebody's in danger every time he moves."

One night he was playing left field in Shea Stadium with Roy McMillan at short when somebody hit a pop fly in that direction. McMillan, once one of the smoothest shortstops in the game, went back, while Swoboda tore madly in, losing his cap as he ran. Everybody in the ball park except Swoboda knew it was McMillan's ball. Just as McMillan took it, Swoboda, apparently trying to get out of the way at the last minute, dove and caught McMillan squarely across the back of his legs. They both went down, but McMillan held the ball.

The next day on the bench I asked McMillan, "Do you think that kid in left field will shorten your career?"

"I don't know if he'll shorten my career or not," McMillan replied, "but he may make me cover a lot less territory."

From then on McMillan didn't seem to go out into left field for fly balls anywhere nearly so far as he had before.

Swoboda's first major-league home run, at Shea Stadium against Houston, was a mammoth shot that cleared the left-field fence and the bullpen and landed in the parking lot beyond. Ken MacKenzie, himself a former Met, had been warming up with Coach Clint Courtney. When they saw the ball go by, they thought someone had thrown it from left field because it didn't seem possible that anyone could hit it that far. After they retrieved the ball they figured it had traveled more than 550 feet.

The first time the Mets went to San Francisco, Swoboda was fascinated by Willie Mays. "I just can't keep my eyes off that man," he remarked before the game as he watched Mays work out in the outfield.

I doubt if any outfielder who ever lived could play ground balls with men on bases the way Mays does. He charges them like an infielder, scoops them up with one hand, then throws the ball in with the deadly accuracy of a good shortstop throwing to first. Swoboda's eyes popped watching him.

Later on that trip, in Milwaukee, the Braves had the bases loaded when the batter hit a hot grounder right down the middle. Swoboda, playing center field that night, came charging in just as he had seen Mays do. As he approached the ball, he bent down and, with a sweeping motion just like Mays's, he reached with his gloved hand while cocking his right hand to throw. The motion was absolutely beautiful. The only trouble was, he didn't touch the ball. It went all the way to the fence, and three runs scored.

"We gotta stop him from watchin' so many of them people," Casey said.

Nothing scared Swoboda. If he thought he could catch a ball, he ran blindly to where he expected it to come down, and I mean blindly. One night in Cincinnati, Frank Robinson of the Reds blasted a shot to left that was out of the ball park from the minute it left the bat. The only one who didn't know it was Swoboda. There's an incline sloping to the wall in deep left at Crosley Field. Outfielders play at the base of it, so they know their first step backward will be up. Swoboda played halfway up it. When Robinson hit the ball, Swoboda started running to his right along the incline. He fell flat on his face and was still there as the drive cleared the fence.

In St. Louis the Mets had a 7–2 lead at the bottom of the ninth when the Cardinals started a rally. They scored two runs to make it 7–4, then filled the bases with two out when Dal Maxvill lofted a lazy fly ball to right, where Swoboda was playing. It looked like a routine out and the end of the ball game, but it wasn't. Swoboda settled under it, suddenly realized he was in the wrong place, made a last-minute stab, missed, and the ball rolled to the fence. By the time he recovered it, Maxvill was on third and three runs were in, tying the score. The Cards won in extra innings.

It's not unusual for the parents of ballplayers to come to watch them play, but Swoboda's mother, who lived in Baltimore, once actually traveled with the club. She went to Chicago for a series with the Cubs. Ron then got permission for her to go to Philadelphia on the club's chartered plane.

Met fans went crazy about him. Whatever he did, right or wrong, brought forth the same wild cheers that Throneberry had drawn. On Banner Day somebody came out with a slogan that said: SWOBODA IS STRONGER THAN DIRT.

His fame spread across the country. One day in Los Angeles a group of beautiful girls came to the ball park to present crates of peaches to the Dodgers as a publicity stunt. The press agent with them came up to me and said, "They're glad to see the Dodgers, but the man they really want to meet is Swoboda." I made everybody, including Swoboda, happy by seeing that they did.

Despite his awkwardness and his mistakes, Swoboda has a chance to be an outstanding star. He messed up some easy plays, but he also made some great ones. He cost the Mets some ball games, but he saved them some others. He can run and throw and hit, and he has made some spectacular catches. He is big and muscular and strong and good-natured. He is Ozark Ike and Lil Abner, Clint Hartung and Smead Jolley and Marv Throneberry, but with a touch of Willie Mays and Ty Cobb.

Ron Swoboda is the Mets.

Chapter 15

So You Want to Start a Ball Club

WHY have the Mets been so bad for so long? Why did they finish a dead last in each of their first four years of existence? Why weren't they able to do better than any of the other three big-league expansion teams, Houston in the National League and Washington and Los Angeles in the American? Why are they such paragons of frustration? Do they like being the worst team in the majors? Do they intend to stay that way indefinitely? Is it true, as some cynics have said, that their fans would leave them flat if they advanced to mediocrity?

Sound, sensible questions. Hardly a day goes by that someone doesn't ask me one, if not all, of them. I can't answer any of them positively, and I doubt if anyone can. We all have theories and opinions of our own, and I'm no exception.

I think the easiest question to answer is why the Mets never

164

finished higher than tenth in the four years Casey Stengel managed them. The reason is they couldn't beat Houston, the other expansion team in their league. Don't ask me why. All I know is they won only three games from the Colt .45s, as the Astros were then called, and lost thirteen in 1962, won five and lost thirteen in 1963, won four and lost fourteen in 1965. Only in 1964, when each won nine games, could the Mets break even with a ball club which figured to be just as poor as they were.

Another reason for the Mets' lack of early success—and this was also true of Houston, which finished eighth once and ninth since—is the remarkable balance enjoyed by the National League. Except for the two expansion teams and the Chicago Cubs, every club in the National League is always a threat to win the pennant. Between 1958 and 1965 there were six different champions. The seventh team, the Phillies, who last won in 1950, lost the 1964 pennant on the final day of the season, after leading the league almost all year.

The better balanced the league, the worse it is for an expansion team because the soft spots are few and far between. There were none for the Mets. Every series was a life-and-death struggle. In the American League, generally dominated by the Yankees, the balance was nowhere nearly so good, with the result that the expansion teams were more successful. They both trailed the rest of the league, in ninth and tenth places, only once in their first five years. The 1962 Angels were third and for a time even pennant contenders.

The Mets are still a long way from third, but perhaps not so far from being in contention as people think. They have some fine young ballplayers, with more on the way. But building a contender today is not the fairly simple job it once was. In the old days you could buy your way into the first division. Money means nothing any more, for every team has plenty of it.

Right from the beginning the Mets have had lots of money,

quickly and easily available. They are not a corporate-owned organization whose actual leaders are far away in some Wall Street ivory tower. You can find the principal owner, the minority owners, the chairman of the board, and the president at almost every home game. They all have money, which they would gladly spend to improve the fortunes of the team.

But on what? Thirty years ago owner Tom Yawkey of the Boston Red Sox could buy the better part of a big-league ball club from owner Connie Mack of the Philadelphia Athletics. Yawkey had money but no players. Mack had players but no money. They had no trouble getting together. But now everyone wants players. The Mets were starving for them, because they had none at all. They were starting from scratch.

How do you go about building a big-league ball club from scratch? Well, to begin with, you take whatever players are available in the expansion draft. You pick and choose and select and weed out and decide on the basis of your scouting reports. And where do you get the scouting reports? From a staff you must put together from the best talent-hunters available.

You soon learn that it doesn't really matter much which players you take from the expansion pool. None of them is very good, or he wouldn't be in it. A man goes into this pool only after his talents have been thoroughly discussed and evaluated by a staff of baseball men more closely associated with him than anybody else—and they have found him wanting. There is something wrong with him, or they wouldn't be willing to give him up.

You know this, so all you can do is hope perhaps there's an undiscovered gem that has been mistakenly passed over. The chances of that are slim indeed. Every ballplayer is so carefully screened that such a slip is nearly impossible. If he's a veteran who once was a star, he might rise to his old heights occasionally, but his former team's judgment that he's through is pretty accurate.

The stories of the players themselves are so much the same they sound like a litany. The veterans say, "I think I have a few good years left. I think I can make up in knowledge and experience what I might have lost in speed. I think I can help this club." The kids say, "I know I can help this club. I know I can play in the majors. I've just never had a chance. Where I was, I was an extra man who sat on the bench all the time. Now that I can play every day, I'll prove I can make it."

You hope these fellows are right, but you soon discover they're not. If your ball club ever makes it, it won't be with them. They will go through the motions and play out your games until you grow your own players, but they won't win for you. They are only fill-ins, either has-beens or never-will-bes, and they will do nothing but add to your frustration.

If you are the Mets, you try immediately to better your personnel. One of your $125,000 choices will be traded away before spring training. Lee Walls, taken off the Phillies roster, will go to the Dodgers along with a bundle of cash for infielder Charley Neal. As the Dodger second baseman, Neal was the star of the 1959 World Series, only three years ago. He's just thirty-one and ought to be in the prime of his career. He should help you, shouldn't he?

But the Dodgers know something you don't know. They know that Charley Neal is all through. There will be days when he will show his old sparkle, but these will come less and less often. Neal will play second base and shortstop and third base, but he won't help you. After a while you begin to wonder how old he *really* is. Finally, in July of 1963, you trade him and a catcher named Sammy Taylor to the Reds for Jesse Gonder. Both Neal and Taylor are soon out of the majors.

You buy Frank Thomas from the Braves and in the deal give up Gus Bell, one of your expansion-draft choices. Thomas can hit for distance, especially in the Polo Grounds, and that first season of 1962 he smashes an amazing 34 home runs. But the

next season his total drops to 15, and you learn that, although
Thomas still has some talents, they are diminishing talents. He's
going the wrong direction for a team that's trying to build. In
August of 1964 you trade him to the Phillies for Wayne
Graham, an infielder, and Gary Kroll, a pitcher. They're young
and you hope they will help, but they don't. At least you haven't
lost anything. Thomas didn't help either.

You have Don Zimmer, an infielder for whom you paid the
Cubs $125,000 in the expansion draft. He has already had a
career with the Dodgers. In spring training he knocks the cover
off the ball. Nobody can get him out. When the season starts
he can't buy a hit. In May you trade him to Cincinnati for a
third baseman named Cliff Cook and a pitcher named Bob
Miller—the second pitching Bob Miller on your club. The
twenty-six-year-old Cook has been the most valuable player in
the American Association, but he has a bad back. Miller has
been a $100,000 bonus pitcher for the Detroit Tigers, but he
didn't pan out for them or for the Reds, and he doesn't pan
out for you.

You have three first basemen: Gil Hodges, Jim Marshall, and
Ed Bouchee. You try to use one to improve your position, but
Marshall is the only one anyone else will take. You trade him
to the Pirates for pitcher Wilmer (Vinegar Bend) Mizell, who
has had great years with the Cardinals as well as with the
Pirates. But that's all over. One day you watch Mizell throwing
in the bullpen. Every time he throws, his cap falls off. He comes
overhand, loses his cap, reaches down, retrieves the cap, slaps
it on his head, then goes through it all over again. You suddenly realize the cap moves almost as fast as the ball. Vinegar
Bend has had it.

You know by now you can't build a winner out of veterans
nobody else wants. You can't even deal them off profitably, for
you're dealing from weakness and everyone else is dealing from
strength. Your men who once had class have nothing much any

more. They're all like Wilmer Mizell. They've had it.

So you turn to kids, but kids don't develop overnight. You have to grow them. There is a senior at James Monroe High School in the Bronx who has broken the home-run records set at that school by Hank Greenberg. His name is Eddie Kranepool, and almost every club in the majors is after him. You camp on his doorstep, offer him a big bonus, and sell him by telling him he can reach the majors faster with the Mets than with any other club.

You are right. On opening day of 1962 Eddie Kranepool played hookey from school to watch the Mets play the Pirates at the Polo Grounds. On opening day of 1963 Eddie Kranepool is back at the Polo Grounds, but this time he doesn't have to play hookey to get there. He's in right field for the Mets and third in Casey Stengel's batting order. He must spend a couple of years in the minors, but by 1965 he's your regular first baseman. He's on the National League All-Star squad.

You make a deal with Milwaukee to buy a second baseman from Austin in the Texas League. Your scouts think he has a chance. He has. His name is Ron Hunt, and by 1964 he's the best second baseman in the National League. That was an unexpected break.

In 1963 you bring everyone you can into spring training, including a twenty-two-year-old southpaw pitcher named Grover Powell. What did Powell ever do? Well, he split the 1962 season between Syracuse in the International League and Auburn in the New York–Pennsylvania League. The International is Class Triple A, the New York–Penn Class D. Powell had almost identical records in both leagues: won two, lost six in each; a 5.79 earned-run average at Syracuse, a 5.12 ERA at Auburn.

This boy is no barn-burner, but at least he did as well in Triple A as in Class D, so maybe he'll do as well in the big leagues. You bring him north, start him against the Phillies, and he beats them. Wonderful! You've got a good young left-handed pitcher who came right out of nowhere.

He doesn't win another game for you. One day he hurts his arm combing his hair. "Greasy kid stuff," says Stengel. That's the end of Grover Powell.

After two years it's obvious that building a big-league team from scratch is a much tougher job than anyone thought, so a special draft is arranged for you and for Houston. You know you're not going to get much from it. You know the only players in expansion drafts are the ones nobody wants. You're tempted to pass it up altogether, but you must do what you can to help your ball club. You finally pick up pitcher Jack Fisher from the Giants.

You're on a treadmill, fighting to keep up with the rest of the league and trying to build at the same time. There's no time out for regrouping. You don't get to rest at the end of an inning, or of a game, or of a season, or of a year. You want to say, "Wait a minute—wait a minute. Give me time to grow some ballplayers." But you don't have any time. You have to put a team on the field every day during the season.

You don't get any help from anybody. You're an orphan in the street. Maybe that's part of your fan appeal. Sometimes you wish you were less a syndrome and more a winner.

You get some bad breaks. You have a young outfielder named Paul Blair, the Baltimore Orioles draft him, and he turns out to be one of the top rookies of the year. Carl Willey, perhaps your best pitcher, suffers a multiple jaw fracture when hit by a line drive off the bat of Gates Brown of the Tigers in an exhibition game. Ron Hunt, your great second baseman, shows up in 1965 spring training with a finger injury he picked up playing handball during the winter, then gets a shoulder separation in a baseline collision with Phil Gagliano of the Cardinals. An operation puts him on the shelf most of the season.

You obtain Dennis Ribant, a right-handed pitcher from the Braves organization whom everyone is after, and he pitches a four-hit shutout over the Pirates nine days after he joins you. Great! You're in business. So what happens? Ribant wins only one more game for you in the next two years.

You make a move every time you see a chance for the slightest improvement. You started with twenty-two players from the original expansion draft. You've tried with veterans on their last time around, pitchers like Frank Lary and Tom Sturdivant and Clem Labine. You've tried with outstanding stars like Gil Hodges and Duke Snider and Warren Spahn and Yogi Berra and Gene Woodling. You've tried with players of limited talent from other clubs, men like Al Moran and Pumpsie Green from the Red Sox, Amado Samuel from the Braves, Larry Elliott from the Pirates. You've had catchers by the dozen—Hobie Landrith, Choo Choo Coleman, Joe Ginsburg, Harry Chiti, Sammy Taylor, Hawk Taylor, Jesse Gonder, Chris Cannizzaro. Some can catch and can't hit. Some can hit and can't catch. Some can't do either. All but Cannizzaro move on. Now you have Johnny Stephenson out of William Carey College in Hattiesburg, Mississippi, and Greg Goosen, whom you drafted from the Dodgers. They're young. They're your hope for the future.

You get a real good break when you buy Roy McMillan from the Braves—a shortstop, a veteran with class, still one of the finest fielders in the game after fifteen years of major league play. There's hardly a bone in his body that hasn't been broken at one time or another, but he steadies your infield. No longer a great star, but he's a big help.

You buy Charlie Smith from the Chicago White Sox. He's been around—from the Dodgers to the Phillies to the White Sox, and now you have him. Always showed promise, even flashes of brilliance, but never quite made it. He looks good at third base, and for a while you think he has finally turned the corner because he has stretches of fine hitting. But after mid-season he's a strikeout king, and Charlie Smith turns out to be no better for you than he was for the White Sox or the Phillies or the Dodgers.

You get pitcher Tracy Stallard from the Red Sox for Felix Mantilla, and he does pretty well. You trade Stallard to the Cardinals for Johnny Lewis and Gordon Richardson. You trade Roger Craig to the Cardinals for George Altman and Bill Wakefield. You trade Altman to the Cubs for Billy Cowan. You trade Cowan to the Braves for a couple of youngsters. This is the way it goes when you're trying to build a big-league team from scratch. You trade and trade and buy and buy and lose and lose, but you never stop hoping.

You reach an important milestone when you get Ken Boyer from the Cardinals for Charlie Smith and Al Jackson in November of 1965. Boyer is an established star, only one year removed from the league's Most Valuable Player. He won it in 1964 when he led the Cardinals to a pennant and world's championship. He tailed off in 1965, but he still rates as a star.

How did you get him? Let Casey Stengel answer. "It's the first time we had some men they wanted," he says from his home in Glendale. The Cardinals wanted Charlie Smith and Al Jackson. They still have hopes for Smith. Jackson is a good left-handed pitcher, one of the last Met survivors of the original expansion draft. Twice he won eight games and lost twenty. Believe it or not, it takes a good pitcher to lose twenty games.

This time you were treated as an equal, not a poor relation. This time you got something for something. This time it was the other team, not you, that traded from weakness. The Cardinals needed a southpaw pitcher so badly they were willing to give up a great third baseman to get one. They had to have Charlie Smith too, because in losing Boyer they needed protection at third base.

You want to keep losing and keep being just a syndrome?

You sure don't! You think you'll lose your fans if you advance to mediocrity or better? Certainly not! Look what happened to the Dodgers. They were as bad as you, a syndrome just like you. Then they became a great ball club, and their fans stayed right with them for years, even after they left Brooklyn. And your fans will stay with you in victory, just as they did in defeat.

Only how do you achieve victory? Where is your future? In the kids, of course, in the Kranepools and the Hunts and the Swobodas and the Napoleons. A few have come of age as big-leaguers already. You hope more will, kids like Kevin Collins and Darrell Sutherland and Tug McGraw and Johnny Lewis and Jim Bethke and Dick Selma and Larry Bearnarth and Jerry Hinsley and Ron Locke and Johnny Stephenson and Greg Goosen and a whole crop of others you haven't heard of yet.

Twenty of your original twenty-two expansion-draft ball-players are gone. Only Jim Hickman and Chris Cannizzaro are left. Your original manager, Casey Stengel, is gone, driven out by age and a broken hip. Now he's chief of Met scouting operations on the West Coast. All of your five original coaches are gone. Cookie Lavagetto is a Giant coach. Solly Hemus manages a Met farm club. Red Ruffing is out of the majors. Rogers Hornsby and Red Kress are dead. The Polo Grounds, your original ball park, is gone, replaced by a sparkling new stadium.

And you're still building. It's different now, though. You have learned so much in four years. Building a ball club was like an infantry battle in the Hürtgen Forest in Germany. You sent in fresh troops, and when you saw them again they were battered and bitter and their skills were dulled and diminished. You had to move forward, so you sent in more fresh troops. You didn't move fast or far, but you kept moving. And you kept sending in more fresh troops. And you kept trying.

That's all you can do now. Keep trying.

Chapter 16

"There Goes Lindsey Nelson"

DURING the two-year run of the New York World's Fair, the Goodyear Tire and Rubber Company based its two blimps at the Flushing Airport in Queens. Millions of people have seen these blimps in various parts of the country, for Goodyear moves them to wherever large crowds gather. As a public-relations gesture, the company often takes passengers up on regularly scheduled runs.

We got so used to the blimps floating lazily in the sky on summer afternoons that they seemed part of the landscape, a spectacular yet soothing sort of sight against the background of the Manhattan skyline. The drone of the motors ebbed and flowed as one or the other of the ships approached the stadium, sometimes hovering high overhead so the passengers could get a panoramic view of the ball game. They never stayed long and never came too low.

And I never thought much about them until one August afternoon in 1965 when I noticed Joe Gallagher staring at them with a gleam in his eye. I had seen that gleam before—the first time he saw the gondola under the roof of the Astrodome.

A blimp has a gondola too, the undercarriage in which the pilot and passengers ride. It's much smaller than the huge balloon overhead that keeps it afloat, but it's big enough to handle six people, or, perhaps, four people and a television camera. I had, in fact, seen cameras in those very blimps. NBC sometimes used them for such spectacular events as the Bing Crosby golf tournament and the Tournament of Roses parade.

But only cameras. Never announcers. Nobody thought of putting an announcer into a Goodyear blimp until Joe Gallagher got the idea on that sunny afternoon in August.

"Lindsey," he said, "you're an experienced gondola man."

"Yeah," I said. "I've been in gondolas twice—in Houston and in Venice. I liked the one in Venice better."

" 'Y'know, you ought to go up first on a Saturday night and give us the whole picture of the fair and the stadium and Manhattan, with the blinking, flashing lights and all."

"Yeah," I said.

"Then you can do it all over again by daylight Sunday afternoon. Altogether different picture."

"Yeah."

"And we'll be the first broadcast team ever to do audio from the gondola of a blimp."

"Yeah."

"As a matter of fact," Joe said, "I've already arranged for you to take a test run in the blimp tomorrow afternoon. Just stop by Flushing Airport on your way to the ball park. They're expecting you at four-thirty in the afternoon."

"Okay," I said.

I had never been up in a blimp, but Ralph Kiner had. "It's a strange feeling," he said. "As long as there's no wind, it's a nice smooth ride with less motion than a rocking chair. But when the wind comes up it tilts and lurches, and then it's landed in a series of descents that you think will be short but really aren't. You'll have a lot of fun."

"I'll bet," I said.

When I checked into the shack at Flushing Airport, a crew was waiting for me. After explaining that they hadn't been able to fly much that day because of the wind but maybe they could give it a try just for me, the boys took me in a station wagon to the pad where the blimp was anchored by sandbags, weights, and men hanging on to ropes.

You get into the gondola by a metal ladder, an easy climb in calm weather but quite a trick when the wind is blowing, as it was that day. The ladder was swinging back and forth, and so was the blimp, but, with the ground crew pushing me from below and the pilot pulling from above, I managed to flop into the gondola.

The pilot was staring at the wind gauge and calling out numbers, which got higher and higher. Finally he turned to me and said, "There's a twenty-five-mile-an-hour wind. We'd better not try it. We could get up all right, but we'd have trouble getting back."

"So there won't be any misunderstanding," I said, "I wish to state here and now that, in any trip I make in this contraption, getting back is a primary consideration."

Then, without help from anyone, I scrambled out of the gondola, down the ladder, into the station wagon, back to the shack, into my own car, and off to Shea Stadium. There I hastily reported to Joe Gallagher that, much as I wanted to go up, it was impossible because of the wind. We went on the road a few days later, so I figured that was the end of the blimp experiment.

But one night several weeks later, with the Giants in town for a weekend series, Gallagher said, "Stop by Flushing Airport on your way to the park tomorrow and they'll take you up on a test run."

This time the weather was perfect. A man and his wife and two children went up with us and we had a wonderful ride, a delightful tour of the North Shore of Long Island with its lovely estates. At one point we hovered over Throg's Neck Bridge, and, at another, directly above the stadium. After an uneventful landing, I was all ready for the real thing, scheduled for the following night.

But that was called off on account of the wind. It seemed just as windy when I left home to drive to the ball park Sunday morning. One blimp was aloft, bouncing around like a cork on a stormy sea, and when nobody said anything on my arrival at the stadium, I figured we weren't going to make it. I was in the press room having lunch with Russ Hodges and Lon Simmons, the Giant broadcasters, when Joe Gallagher came in and said, "There's a fellow downstairs with a car to drive you to Flushing Airport. We're going to give it a try."

As we approached the airport, the blimp I had seen earlier came down, and I met its pilot at the shack.

"How is it?" I said.

"Windy," he said. "It's sure great to be back on the ground."

I gulped all the way to the blimp. It was swaying back and forth, and so was the ladder. The door of the gondola was almost completely filled by a television camera mounted on a platform, with a monitor set behind it. Two engineers from station WOR-TV and the pilot were waiting for me as I clambered aboard.

"Pretty windy, isn't it?" I ventured.

"Oh, well," said the pilot. "We've gone this far. We might as well go the rest of the way."

We shot up like a rocket, but once we were airborne it wasn't too bad—bumpy but comfortable enough. We went over the stadium, and when we arrived the game was already in progress.

I could see the field clearly, but we were much too high to make out any details. The monitor was working nicely, though, and I could follow the game on that.

On my headset I heard Bob Murphy say, "And now we're going to check with our colleague, Lindsey Nelson, who is in the Goodyear blimp above Shea Stadium. Can you hear us, Lindsey?"

"Yes, Bob," I said, "I can hear you very clearly."

"I say, Lindsey," Murph repeated, "can you hear us?"

"Very well."

"Can you hear us?"

I could hear Murph, but he couldn't hear me. "Just keep talking," one of the engineers said. "We'll check out the equipment and try to get this thing going."

So I kept talking. I talked about Manhattan, and New Jersey across the Hudson, and Westchester County to the north, and Shea Stadium, and how small everybody on the field looked, and about the crowd, and about the World's Fair, and about La Guardia, and about everything else I could think of. And not a soul heard me—absolutely nobody. It was too noisy in the gondola for the engineers and the pilot to hear me, and I wasn't transmitting to anywhere.

Every so often Murph or Ralph, whoever was on the air, repeated, "Can you hear me, Lindsey?" and I said, "Very well," and nothing happened. I could hear all too well. The Mets were getting their brains beaten out.

The engineer tapped me on the shoulder and nodded, indicating that we were finally transmitting. We could get through with an audio report at last. We were right over the stadium, but I might as well have been in Stamford, for all I could see. The ballplayers looked like ants. There wasn't a chance of announcing the game by watching them move around from where I sat.

However, the television monitor was perfect. Everything was so clear that I could broadcast from that, and listeners would never know the difference. There was only one small problem. The way our gear was lashed up, I had to press a mike button to talk, and every time I did that the picture on the monitor went off. I'd have to talk fast and in small doses and, if I missed anything, just hope I could get a clue from watching the figures on the field far below.

Suddenly Joe Gallagher said, "Lindsey, you're on. Try doing a play-by-play."

As he spoke, the blimp drifted away from the field. We were over the parking lot, behind the horseshoe end of the stadium, and I couldn't see anything but automobiles, the World's Fair, and a panoramic view of Manhattan and its surroundings. I stared at the monitor and pressed the mike button.

"Haller up for the Giants," I said. Only Haller had disappeared, so I quickly released the button. A pitch came in and the umpire raised his right arm.

Down went the button and out went the picture as I said, "Strike one, called." Then I quickly released the button. Haller was still there. Somehow or other, I managed to get through Haller and Lanier without losing the ball game.

"Fuentes comes up for the Giants," I said, not because I saw Fuentes but because I knew he was due up next. When I took my finger off the button, Fuentes was standing in the batter's box.

I felt a sinking sensation and, without my hand touching the mike button, the ball game disappeared. Just then the pilot yelled over the roar of the motor, "Oops, sorry!"

"The picture's gone," I howled. "What happened?"

"See that jet over there?" he said.

I nodded. There was a big transport plane coming down a few miles off to our right.

"Well, if I hadn't pulled the picture plugs and dropped," he said, "you'd be seeing it a lot better. In fact, you might be in it."

He replaced the plugs, and the picture came on again. After that, except for an occasional pause when I tried to figure out what I might have missed while the picture was off, things moved smoothly enough. I heard later that the response of the fans was terrific. Right from the moment I first went on the air, the telephone switchboard was jammed as people called in to tell us what they thought of the broadcast. Some objected, but most liked it. One caller asked for Ralph Kiner. Told he was on the air, the man said, "I just wanted to tell him that Lindsey fell out of the blimp."

I did a couple of innings, and the word finally came for us to go down. After I signed off, all the transmitting and picture plugs were pulled, and we headed for Flushing Airport.

Lon Simmons was on the air, broadcasting the game back to San Francisco. He and Russ Hodges had both been keeping their listeners informed on the blimp's progress, making frequent references to the fact that I was aboard to broadcast the game to Met fans.

As the blimp moved out of Lon's sight in the gathering shadows, he told his Giant fans back home, "And there goes Lindsey Nelson, sinking slowly in the West."

Now I wanna tell ya about that. . . .